INTRODUCING
ISSUES WITH
OPPOSING
VIEWPOINTS®

Impeachment

Lisa Idzikowski, Book Editor

GREENHAVEN
PUBLISHING

Published in 2022 by Greenhaven Publishing, LLC
353 3rd Avenue, Suite 255, New York, NY 10010

Articles in Greenhaven Publishing anthologies are often edited for length to meet page requirements. In addition, original titles of these works are changed to clearly present the main thesis and to explicitly indicate the author's opinion. Every effort is made to ensure that Greenhaven Publishing accurately reflects the original intent of the authors. Every effort has been made to trace the owners of the copyrighted material.

Library of Congress Cataloging-in-Publication Data

Names: Idzikowski, Lisa, editor.
Title: Impeachment / Lisa Idzikowski, book editor.
Description: First edition. | New York, NY : Greenhaven Publishing, LLC,
    2022. | Series: Introducing issues with opposing viewpoints | Includes
    bibliographical references and index. | Audience: Ages 12–15
    | Audience: Grades 7–9 | Summary: "The viewpoints in this volume examine
    impeachment, offer interpretations of the Founding Fathers' intentions,
    and question whether there is a better way"— Provided by publisher.
Identifiers: LCCN 2020056710 | ISBN 9781534508071 (library binding) | ISBN
    9781534508064 (paperback)
Subjects: LCSH: Impeachments—United States—Juvenile literature. |
    Presidents—United States—Juvenile literature. | United
    States—Politics and government—Juvenile literature. | Trump, Donald,
    1946—Impeachment—Juvenile literature.
Classification: LCC KF5075 . I468 2022 | DDC 342.73/068—dc23
LC record available at https://lccn.loc.gov/2020056710

Manufactured in the United States of America

Website: http://greenhavenpublishing.com

Contents

Chapter 3: Should the Impeachment Process Be Changed?

Foreword

Indulging in a wide spectrum of ideas, beliefs, and perspectives is a critical cornerstone of democracy. After all, it is often debates over differences of opinion, such as whether to legalize abortion, how to treat prisoners, or when to enact the death penalty, that shape our society and drive it forward. Such diversity of thought is frequently regarded as the hallmark of a healthy and civilized culture. As Reverend Clifford Schutjer of the First Congregational Church in Mansfield, Ohio, declared in a 2001 sermon, "Surrounding oneself with only like-minded people, restricting what we listen to or read only to what we find agreeable is irresponsible. Refusing to entertain doubts once we make up our minds is a subtle but deadly form of arrogance." With this advice in mind, Introducing Issues with Opposing Viewpoints books aim to open readers' minds to the critically divergent views that comprise our world's most important debates.

Introducing Issues with Opposing Viewpoints simplifies for students the enormous and often overwhelming mass of material now available via print and electronic media. Collected in every volume is an array of opinions that captures the essence of a particular controversy or topic. Introducing Issues with Opposing Viewpoints books embody the spirit of nineteenth-century journalist Charles A. Dana's axiom: "Fight for your opinions, but do not believe that they contain the whole truth, or the only truth." Absorbing such contrasting opinions teaches students to analyze the strength of an argument and compare it to its opposition. From this process readers can inform and strengthen their own opinions, or be exposed to new information that will change their minds. Introducing Issues with Opposing Viewpoints is a mosaic of different voices. The authors are statesmen, pundits, academics, journalists, corporations, and ordinary people who have felt compelled to share their experiences and ideas in a public forum. Their words have been collected from newspapers, journals, books, speeches, interviews, and the internet, the fastest growing body of opinionated material in the world.

Introducing Issues with Opposing Viewpoints shares many of the well-known features of its critically acclaimed parent series, Opposing Viewpoints. The articles allow readers to absorb and compare divergent perspectives. Active reading questions preface each viewpoint, requiring the student to approach the material thoughtfully and carefully. Photographs, charts, and graphs supplement each article. A thorough introduction provides readers with crucial background on an issue. An annotated bibliography points the reader toward articles, books, and websites that contain additional information on the topic. An appendix of organizations to contact contains a wide variety of charities, nonprofit organizations, political groups, and private enterprises that each hold a position on the issue at hand. Finally, a comprehensive index allows readers to locate content quickly and efficiently.

Introducing Issues with Opposing Viewpoints is also significantly different from Opposing Viewpoints. As the series title implies, its presentation will help introduce students to the concept of opposing viewpoints and learn to use this material to aid in critical writing and debate. The series' four-color, accessible format makes the books attractive and inviting to readers of all levels. In addition, each viewpoint has been carefully edited to maximize a reader's understanding of the content. Short but thorough viewpoints capture the essence of an argument. A substantial, thought-provoking essay question placed at the end of each viewpoint asks the student to further investigate the issues raised in the viewpoint, compare and contrast two authors' arguments, or consider how one might go about forming an opinion on the topic at hand. Each viewpoint contains sidebars that include at-a-glance information and handy statistics. A Facts About section located in the back of the book further supplies students with relevant facts and figures.

Following in the tradition of the Opposing Viewpoints series, Greenhaven Publishing continues to provide readers with invaluable exposure to the controversial issues that shape our world. As John Stuart Mill once wrote: "The only way in which a human being can make some approach to knowing the whole of a subject is by hearing what can be said about it by persons of every variety of opinion and studying all modes in which it can be looked at by every character of mind. No wise man ever acquired his wisdom in any mode but this." It is to this principle that Introducing Issues with Opposing Viewpoints books are dedicated.

Introduction

*"The President, Vice President and all Civil Officers of the
United States, shall be removed from Office on Impeachment
for, and Conviction of, Treason, Bribery, or other high Crimes
and Misdemeanors."*
— US Constitution, Article II, Section 4

The years surrounding 2020 will go down in history for a number of reasons. People will obviously remember dealing with a worldwide pandemic. But what of the impeachment of US president Donald J. Trump, which began just a month earlier, in December 2019? Will people recall the constant news reports? Will people recall the division of the country? Will people recall how they felt when the US Senate voted, essentially declaring Trump not guilty as charged by the Democrat-controlled House of Representatives? And will they remember how the president later said he was "totally vindicated" and free and clear of the charges of misconduct?

The impeachment was a hot topic. People everywhere discussed and debated the issue. Older students most likely studied the topic in school. Young children might not have understood what was happening, but perhaps they sensed a different kind of stress affecting the adults in their lives. Impeachment certainly has meant different things to different people, and because of various impeachments throughout US history, there are common misconceptions about its true definition. According to Merriam Webster, to impeach someone is "to charge a public official formally with misconduct in office," or "to charge (a public official) before a competent tribunal (as the US Senate) with misconduct in office."

At the Constitutional Convention of 1787 in Pennsylvania's State House (presently Constitution Hall), representatives debated the issue of impeachment and how it should be written into the Constitution. Well-known and well-regarded, Benjamin Franklin offered his ideas: "What was the practice before in cases where the chief magistrate rendered himself obnoxious?" He dismissed the idea of assassination but said, "It would be the best way therefore to provide in the

Constitution for the regular punishment of the Executive where his misconduct should deserve it, and for his honorable acquittal when he should be unjustly accused." Another Founding Father, James Madison, who later became America's fourth president, agreed that something had to be written into the Constitution because a president "might lose his capacity after his appointment. He might pervert his administration into a scheme of peculation or oppression. He might betray his trust to foreign powers." After much debate, the convention came to an agreement and by that fall had approved the final draft of the Constitution, which included Section 4 of Article II (noted earlier in the introductory quote), which detailed the outcome of impeachment and the actions that would lead to the process.

Interestingly, impeachment is not a process limited to long ago history. It may have its roots in British law, but in the United States, about a few dozen cases have been tried. Donald Trump joins a group of three previous US presidents that have been impeached. President Andrew Johnson and William Jefferson Clinton, like Donald J. Trump, have been acquitted by the US Senate. Richard M. Nixon resigned from office before the vote of impeachment charges against him was carried out.

One might wonder if the process of impeachment causes problems for a country. Some might argue that impeachments are overly political or partisan. Members of one political party might be accused of simply being on a witch hunt against their political opponents, especially if the candidate of the accusing party has lost an election (as in the 2016 US election in which Republican Donald Trump beat Democrat Hillary Clinton). Others might disagree and provide evidence of behavior that warrants the proceedings. In the case of Donald Trump's impeachment, and according to a 2020 poll done by Pew Research, "roughly half of US adults (51%) say the outcome of the Senate trial should be Trump's removal from office, while 46% say the result should lead to Trump remaining in office." Not surprisingly, a majority of Republicans surveyed said that the president should not be removed from office, while almost the same percentage of Democrats (85%) said that Trump should be removed from his post. This split along Republican vs. Democrat lines typically is reflected in the division evident among ordinary citizens. And there was plenty of evidence of this poisonous divide among the US public all throughout Donald Trump's years in office and throughout the 2020 election cycle.

What about the question of fairness or validity? Is the process of impeachment unjust or unfair? As would be expected, this question has its proponents and opponents. Tellingly, a group of more than 800 legal scholars from across the United States signed a letter and sent it to Congress insisting that President Trump engaged in impeachable conduct. They concluded that "his conduct is precisely the type of threat to our democracy that the Founders feared when they included the remedy of impeachment in the Constitution." And furthermore, the experts stated that they were not implying that the president committed a crime but that their standard of judgement "is constitutional; it does not depend on what Congress has chosen to criminalize." Sadly, according to Pew Research, one in five Americans were not too confident that representatives from either major party, Republicans or Democrats, would act fairly during the impeachment trial of the president.

And that was only Trump's first impeachment! Donald J. Trump made history by being the first US president to be impeached twice and to be impeached after leaving office. This second offense was connected to the Capitol riots of January 6, 2021, in which Trump supporters stormed the US Capitol in an attempt to overturn the 2020 presidential election, which Trump had lost. The outgoing president was accused of inciting the insurrectionists. Once again, Americans were split. And once again, Donald J. Trump was acquitted.

Something can and must be done to improve the conditions under which a president, vice president, and other civil officers of the United States can be dealt with under pressing charges now and into the future. A first step might be educating everyone about this controversial topic and realizing how it affects us all. The viewpoints within *Introducing Issues with Opposing Viewpoints: Impeachment* explore the subject from different angles and shed light on this interesting and ongoing contemporary issue.

Chapter 1

What Is the Purpose of Impeachment?

Presidential impeachment is just one kind of impeachment.

There Is a Legal Standard and Procedure for Presidential Impeachment

"There is substantial difference of opinion over the interpretation of these words."

Ronald Arthur Lowry

In the following viewpoint, Ronald Arthur Lowry presents a balanced piece describing the impeachment process. Lowry outlines the Constitutional articles that pertain to impeachment and points out that there is a difference of opinion when it comes to impeachable offenses. He also analyzes the role of the US Supreme Court in the matter of impeachment. Ronald Arthur Lowry is a lawyer and member of the Board of Governors of the State Bar of Georgia.

AS YOU READ, CONSIDER THE FOLLOWING QUESTIONS:
1. According to Lowry, what three reasons justify impeachment?
2. As stated by the author, which part of Congress begins impeachment?
3. Which part of Congress conducts a trial in impeachment cases, according to the author?

"Presidential Impeachment: The Legal Standard and Procedure," by Ronald Arthur Lowry, Thomson Reuters. Reprinted by permission.

The involuntary removal of a sitting President of the United States has never occurred in our history. The only legal way such can be accomplished is by the impeachment process. This article discusses the legal standard to be properly applied by members of the US House of Representatives when voting for or against Articles of Impeachment, and members of the US Senate when voting whether to convict and remove from office a President of the US, as well as the procedure to be followed.

Article I § 2 of the United States Constitution gives the House of Representatives the sole power to impeach (make formal charges against) and Article I § 3 gives the Senate the sole power to try impeachments. Article II § 4 of the Constitution provides as follows:

> *The President, Vice President and all civil officers of the United States, shall be removed from office on impeachment for, and conviction of, treason, bribery, or other high crimes and misdemeanors.*

Thus, the operative legal standard to apply to an impeachment of a sitting President is "treason, bribery, or other high crimes and misdemeanors." There is substantial difference of opinion over the interpretation of these words. There are essentially four schools of thought concerning the meaning of these words, although there are innumerable subsets within those four categories.

Congressional Interpretation

The first general school of thought is that the standard enunciated by the Constitution is subject entirely to whatever interpretation Congress collectively wishes to make:

> *What, then, is an impeachable offense? The only honest answer is that an impeachable offense is whatever a majority of the House of Representatives considers it to be at a given moment in history; conviction results from whatever offense or offenses two-thirds of the other body considers to be sufficiently serious to require removal of the accused from office..." (Congressman Gerald Ford, 116 Cong. Rec. H.3113-3114. April 15, 1970).*

This view has been rejected by most legal scholars because it would have the effect of having the President serve at the pleasure of Congress. However there are some, particularly in Congress, who hold this opinion.

An Indictable Crime

The second view is that the Constitutional standard makes it necessary for a President to have committed an indictable crime in order to be subject to impeachment and removal from office. This view was adopted by many Republicans during the impeachment investigation of President Richard M. Nixon. The proponents of this view point to the tone of the language of Article II § 4 itself, which seems to be speaking in criminal law terms.

There are other places in the Constitution that seem to support this interpretation, as well. For example, Article III § 2 (3) provides that "the trial of all crimes, except in cases of impeachment, shall be by jury." Clearly the implication of this sentence from the Constitution is that impeachment is being treated as a criminal offense, ergo, impeachment requires a criminal offense to have been committed.

Article II § 2 (1) authorizes the President to grant pardons "for offenses against the United States, except in cases of impeachment." This sentence implies that the Framers must have thought impeachment, and the acts which would support impeachment, to be criminal in nature.

In the past, England had used impeachment of the King's ministers as a means of controlling policy (Parliament could not get rid of the King, but could get rid of his ministers who carried out acts Parliament believed to be against the best interest of the country). However, in English impeachments, once convicted that person was not only removed from office but was also punished (usually by execution).

Misdemeanor

The third approach is that an indictable crime is not required to impeach and remove a President. The proponents of this view focus on the word "misdemeanor," which did not have a specific criminal connotation to it at the time the Constitution was ratified. This

LEGISLATIVE

EXECUTIVE

JUDICIAL

Presidential impeachments are carried out by the legislative branch of the US government.

interpretation is somewhat belied by details of the debate the Framers had in arriving at the specific language to be used for the impeachment standard.

Initially the standard was to be "malpractice or neglect of duty." This was removed and replaced with "treason, bribery, or corruption." The word "corruption" was then eliminated. On the floor during debate the suggestion was made to add the term "maladministration." This was rejected as being too vague and the phrase "high crimes and misdemeanors" was adopted in its place. There are many legal scholars who believe this lesser standard is the correct one, however.

Relating to the President's Official Duties
The fourth view is that an indictable crime is not required, but that the impeachable act or acts done by the President must in some way relate to his official duties. The bad act may or may not be a crime but it would be more serious than simply "maladministration." This view is buttressed in part by an analysis of the entire phrase "high crimes or misdemeanors," which seems to be a term of art speaking to a political connection for the bad act or acts. In order to impeach it would not be necessary for the act to be a crime, but not all crimes would be impeachable offenses.

Some hold the opinion that Congress could pass laws by declaring what constitutes "high crimes and misdemeanors," which would, in effect, be a list of impeachable offenses. That has never happened. (Query: If Congress passed such a code of impeachable offenses, could that be applied retroactively, much as a definition, to a sitting President? Would such an application be viewed as an ex post facto law? Also, would such a statue be an attempt to amend the Constitution, without following the amendment procedure?)

How Congress Sets the Rules for Impeachment
Both the US House of Representatives and the US Senate have the right to make their own rules governing their procedure, and to change those rules. Under current rules, the actual impeachment inquiry begins in the Judiciary Committee of the House of Representatives. That Committee holds hearings, takes evidence, and hears testimony

of witnesses concerning matters relevant to the inquiry.
Typically, as occurred in the
case of President Nixon,
there will also be a Minority
Counsel who serves the interest of the party not controlling
Congress.

Witnesses are interrogated
by the Committee Counsel, the Minority Counsel, and each of the
members of the House Judiciary Committee. The Committee formu-
lates Articles of Impeachment, which could contain multiple counts.
The Committee votes on the Articles of Impeachment and the results of
the vote are reported to the House as a whole. The matter is then referred
to the whole House, which debates the matter and votes on the Articles
of Impeachment, which may or may not be changed. If the Articles of
Impeachment are approved, the matter is sent to the Senate for trial.

Impeachment Trials

The trial in the Senate is handled by "Managers" from the House of
Representatives, with the assistance of attorneys employed for the
prosecution of the impeachment case. The Senate sits as a jury. (In
the past the Senate has heard judicial impeachments by appointing
a subcommittee especially for that purpose, which then reports its
findings to the Senate as a whole.) The Senate would then debate
the matter, and vote, each individual Senator voting whether to convict the President and remove him from office, or against conviction. If more than two-thirds of the Senators present vote to convict,
the President would be removed from office. Thus a Senator who
abstained from voting but was present would in effect be voting
against conviction. (Article I § 3).

If the President is convicted by a vote of the Senate, and removed
from office, yet another grave constitutional crisis is then presented.
Does the President have a right of appeal, and if so, to whom? Article
I § 3 of the Constitution states:

The Senate shall have the sole Power to try all Impeachments...

FAST FACT

In the United States, three
presidents have been tried for
impeachment. None has been
found guilty as charged.

For many years, the conventional view was that the forgoing section of the Constitution meant that the Senate was the final arbiter when it came to impeachments (at least as to Federal Judges) and that what constituted an impeachable offense would be unreviewable. See *Ritter v. US*, 84 Ct. Cl. 293 (1936) cert denied 300 US 668 (1937).

However, if there is an impeachment standard (and there can be no doubt that there is as the Constitution specifically establishes one—"treason, bribery or other high crimes and misdemeanors"), then it is only logical that it is possible for that standard not to be correctly followed. If such is the case, who is responsible for saying that the standard was not correctly followed? There can only be one answer—the courts. As there has never been a successful impeachment and removal of a sitting President, there is no authority "on all fours" for the proposition either way. However, there is authority that would shed some light on this complicated question.

The Role of the US Supreme Court

The Supreme Court of the United States has decided that it should not review judicial impeachments, using the "political question" doctrine to sidestep the issue. In the Walter Nixon case—*Walter Nixon v. United States*, 506 US 224 (1993)—Judge Nixon attacked the rule of the Senate allowing a subcommittee to hear evidence, rather than the Senate as a whole, in his judicial impeachment. The opinion of the Supreme Court declined to review Judge Nixon's case, and in dicta is not binding on future Courts.

Even though the Court was unanimous in concluding not to review Judge Nixon's removal from office, there were multiple concurring opinions. The concurring opinion of Justice White indicates an unwillingness, on his part at least, to conclude in advance that a Presidential impeachment would be unreviewable. As stated by Justice White at footnote 3, page 247 of the Walter Nixon case:

> *Finally, as applied to the special case of the President, the majority's argument merely points out that, were the Senate to convict the President without any kind of trial, a Constitutional crisis might well result. It hardly follows that*

the Court ought to refrain from upholding the Constitution in all impeachment cases. Nor does it follow that, in cases of Presidential impeachment, the Justices ought to abandon their constitutional responsibilities because the Senate has precipitated a crisis.

This view is echoed by Justice Souter in his concurring opinion in the same case:

If the Senate were to act in a manner seriously threatening the integrity of its results...judicial interference might well be appropriate. (Walter Nixon v. United States, 506 US at 253.)

EVALUATING THE AUTHOR'S ARGUMENTS:

Viewpoint author Ronald Arthur Lowry describes the legal standard of impeachment in the US. What do you believe constitutes treason, bribery, or other high crimes and misdemeanors as stated in the US Constitution?

Viewpoint 2

"There is no doubt that the Framers saw impeachment as a part of the system of checks and balances to maintain the separation of powers and the republican form of government."

The US Constitution Does Not Specify How to Initiate Impeachment

Stephen B. Presser

In the following viewpoint, Stephen B. Presser defines the process of impeachment in the United States. The author outlines the Constitutional supports behind impeachment and some of the major historical figures that have been impeached. Presser points out that members of the House of Representatives take an oath to uphold the US Constitution and this includes dealing with officials who commit impeachable offenses. Stephen B. Presser is Professor Emeritus of legal history at Northwestern University and author of *Law Professors: Three Centuries of Shaping American Law*.

"Impeachment," by Stephen B. Presser, The Heritage Foundation. Reprinted by permission.

AS YOU READ, CONSIDER THE FOLLOWING QUESTIONS:
1. Who wrote the standards for impeachment, as explained by the author?
2. Which governmental officials have most frequently been subject to impeachment, as stated by the viewpoint article?
3. What happened in the impeachment case against President Richard M. Nixon, according to the viewpoint?

"The House of Representatives ... shall have the sole Power of Impeachment." –Article 1, Section 2, Clause 5. In the debates in the Constitutional Convention, the delegates were attempting to craft a mechanism that would allow for the disciplining of a President who abused his constitutional responsibilities without creating a weapon by which the President would be prevented from carrying them out. At bottom, it was a question of how to refine and make effective the separation of powers.

Article II, Section 4 states that the President, Vice President, and "all civil Officers of the United States"—which includes judges—can be impeached. Members of Congress can be expelled by their own respective body. (See Article I, Section 5, Clause 2.)

Early on, some delegates expressed the apprehension that those serving in the federal government would be disinclined to monitor each other. Accordingly, John Dickinson proposed "that the Executive be made removeable by the National Legislature on the request of a majority of the Legislatures of individual States." James Madison opposed the idea because it would subject the executive to the "intrigues" of the states. After defeating Dickinson's proposal, the members of the Convention also turned aside George Mason's and Gouverneur Morris's initial fears that the impeachment power might render the executive the servant of the legislature. Instead, the Framers opted for the procedure that had been followed by the English and by the constitutions of most of the states. The appropriate place of bringing charges of impeachment, which power is analogous to the bringing of criminal charges by a grand jury, is in the lower house of the legislature. The grand and petit juries are popular institutions, so it made sense to have the branch closest to

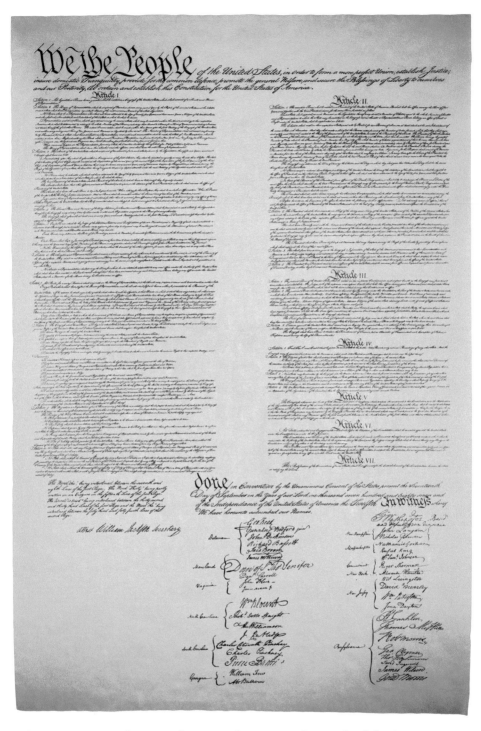

The US Constitution does not outline impeachment proceedings in detail, leaving many details open to interpretation and debate.

the people charged with this indictment-like power.

The Constitution does not specify how impeachment proceedings are to be initiated. Early in our history, a Member would rise on the floor of Congress and propose an impeachment, which

would then be assigned to a committee. In recent years, Members of the House Judiciary Committee have initiated the proceeding and then made recommendations for the whole House's consideration. If the House votes an impeachment resolution, the Chairman of the Judiciary Committee recommends a slate of "managers," whom the House subsequently approves by resolution, and who then become prosecutors in the trial in the Senate.

For a time there was legislation enabling the Attorney General to appoint a "special prosecutor" with the power to recommend impeachments to Congress, but dissatisfaction with the power of such an unchecked independent counsel led to the expiration of the authorizing statute. Even the most famous "independent counsel," Judge Kenneth Starr, who recommended the impeachment of President William Jefferson Clinton to Congress, had consistently argued against the practice of appointing such independent counsels.

There have not been many instances of impeachment over the years—a few dozen in all, mostly of corrupt federal judges. The most notable impeachments—Justice Samuel Chase, and Presidents Andrew Johnson and William Jefferson Clinton—have ended in acquittals by the Senate. There were proceedings and hearings at the House Judiciary Committee and a bill of impeachment reported to the House against President Richard M. Nixon. Nixon resigned before the full House could vote on the impeachment charges against him.

The near-unanimous view of constitutional commentators is that the House of Representatives' "sole power" of impeachment is a political question and therefore not reviewable by the judiciary. The House is constitutionally obligated to base a bill of impeachment on the standards set out in Article II. (See Article II, Section 4.)

However, the fact that the Constitution's text grants the House the "sole power," and the fact that such a review is not clearly within the Article III power of the federal judiciary, indicate that this responsibility is the House's alone. The Supreme Court has found that the Senate's "sole power" to try impeachments is not justiciable. *Nixon v. United States* (1993).

That leaves the question of whether the clause imposes an affirmative duty on the House to monitor the conduct of those subject to impeachment, and, when evidence of impeachable offenses is manifest, to initiate proceedings. It has been the general American practice regarding criminal law to grant considerable discretion to prosecutors, so that by analogy one could argue that the House has complete discretion to decide whether to initiate impeachment proceedings. On the other hand, Alexander Hamilton argued in the Federalist No. 77 that the nation would find "republican" safety from a presidential abuse of power by the mode of his election and by his "being at all times liable to impeachment." There is no doubt that the Framers saw impeachment as a part of the system of checks and balances to maintain the separation of powers and the republican form of government. The implication is that when the President (or other impeachable official) has committed an impeachable offense, the Members of the House, bound by the oaths they take to uphold the Constitution, are under a particular obligation to deal with the miscreant's offenses, irrespective of whether their bill of impeachment may or may not lead to a conviction in the Senate.

EVALUATING THE AUTHOR'S ARGUMENTS:

Viewpoint author Stephen B. Presser outlines impeachment in the United States. Compare this viewpoint with that of Ronald Arthur Lowry. Do the two authors agree or disagree about impeachment? Back up your opinion with a written comparison of the two viewpoints.

The House Has Initiated Impeachment Proceedings More Than 60 Times

"The founders considered impeachment so important that they made it part of the Constitution even before they defined the contours of the presidency."

Office of the Historian, US House of Representatives

In the following viewpoint, the Office of the Historian of the US House of Representatives analyzes the subject of impeachment. The viewpoint provides a concise history of the development of the impeachment process, where the idea originated, what body of individuals cemented it as part of US government, and what offenses constitute an impeachment. The Office of the Historian studies and documents the history of the House of Representatives.

History, Art & Archives, US House of Representatives, "Impeachment," https://history.house.gov/Institution /Origins-Development/Impeachment/. Reprinted by permission.

1. As stated by the viewpoint, when did the debate about impeachment originally take place?
2. Who presides over the impeachment trial, as stated by the viewpoint?
3. How many times through history has the House of Representatives initiated impeachment proceedings, according to the viewpoint?

T he Constitution gives the House of Representatives the sole power to impeach an official, and it makes the Senate the sole court for impeachment trials. The power of impeachment is limited to removal from office but also provides for a removed officer to be disqualified from holding future office. Fines and potential jail time for crimes committed while in office are left to civil courts.

Origins

Impeachment comes from British constitutional history. The process evolved from the 14th century as a way for parliament to hold the king's ministers accountable for their public actions. Impeachment, as Alexander Hamilton of New York explained in Federalist 65, varies from civil or criminal courts in that it strictly involves the "misconduct of public men, or in other words from the abuse or violation of some public trust." Individual state constitutions had provided for impeachment for "maladministration" or "corruption" before the US Constitution was written. And the founders, fearing the potential for abuse of executive power, considered impeachment so important that they made it part of the Constitution even before they defined the contours of the presidency.

Constitutional Framing

During the Federal Constitutional Convention, the framers addressed whether even to include impeachment trials in the Constitution, the venue and process for such trials, what crimes should warrant

Andrew Johnson was the seventeenth president of the United States, assuming office in 1865 after the assassination of Abraham Lincoln. In 1868, Johnson became the first US president to be impeached.

impeachment, and the likelihood of conviction. Rufus King of Massachusetts argued that having the legislative branch pass judgment on the executive would undermine the separation of powers;

better to let elections punish a President. "The Executive was to hold his place for a limited term like the members of the Legislature," King said, so "he would periodically be tried for his behaviour by his electors." Massachusetts's Elbridge Gerry, however, said impeachment was a way to keep the executive in check: "A good magistrate will not fear [impeachments]. A bad one ought to be kept in fear of them."

Another issue arose regarding whether Congress might lack the resolve to try and convict a sitting President. Presidents, some delegates observed, controlled executive appointments that ambitious Members of Congress might find desirable. Delegates to the Convention also remained undecided on the venue for impeachment trials. The Virginia Plan, which set the agenda for the Convention, initially contemplated using the judicial branch. Again, though, the founders chose to follow the British example, where the House of Commons brought charges against officers and the House of Lords considered them at trial. Ultimately, the founders decided that during presidential impeachment trials, the House would manage the prosecution, while the Chief Justice would preside over the Senate during the trial.

The founders also addressed what crimes constituted grounds for impeachment. Treason and bribery were obvious choices, but George Mason of Virginia thought those crimes did not include a large number of punishable offenses against the state. James Madison of Virginia objected to using the term "maladministration" because it was too vague. Mason then substituted "other high Crimes and Misdemeanors" in addition to treason and bribery. The term "high Crimes and Misdemeanors" was a technical term—again borrowed from British legal practice—that denoted crimes by public officials against the government. Mason's revision was accepted without further debate. But subsequent experience demonstrated the revised phrase failed to clarify what constituted impeachable offenses.

The House's Role

The House brings impeachment charges against federal officials as part of its oversight and investigatory responsibilities. Individual Members of the House can introduce impeachment resolutions like ordinary bills, or the House could initiate proceedings by passing a resolution authorizing an inquiry. The Committee on the Judiciary ordinarily has jurisdiction over impeachments, but special committees investigated charges before the Judiciary Committee was created in 1813. The committee then chooses whether to pursue articles of impeachment against the accused official and report them to the full House. If the articles are adopted (by simple majority vote), the House appoints Members by resolution to manage the ensuing Senate trial on its behalf. These managers act as prosecutors in the Senate and are usually members of the Judiciary Committee. The number of managers has varied across impeachment trials but has traditionally been an odd number. The partisan composition of managers has also varied depending on the nature of the impeachment, but the managers, by definition, always support the House's impeachment action.

The Use of Impeachment

The House has initiated impeachment proceedings more than 60 times but less than a third have led to full impeachments. Just eight—all federal judges—have been convicted and removed from office by the Senate. Outside of the 15 federal judges impeached by the House, three Presidents [Andrew Johnson in 1868, William Jefferson (Bill) Clinton in 1998, and Donald J. Trump in 2019 and 2021], a cabinet secretary (William Belknap in 1876), and a US Senator (William Blount of Tennessee in 1797) have also been impeached.

Blount's impeachment trial—the first ever conducted—established the principle that Members of Congress and Senators were not "Civil Officers" under the Constitution, and accordingly, they could only be removed from office by a two-thirds vote for expulsion by their respective chambers. Blount, who had been accused of instigating an insurrection of American Indians to further British interests in Florida, was not convicted, but the Senate did expel him. Other impeachments have featured judges taking the bench when drunk or profiting from their position. The trial of President Johnson, however, focused on whether the President could remove cabinet officers without obtaining Congress's approval. Johnson's acquittal firmly set the precedent—debated from the beginning of the nation—that the President may remove appointees even if they required Senate confirmation to hold office.

EVALUATING THE AUTHOR'S ARGUMENTS:

In this viewpoint, the Archive of the US House of Representatives explores the origin of the process of impeachment and how it was created. Why do you suppose that America's founders were so intent upon having the process of impeachment? Support your opinion with evidence from the viewpoint article.

Viewpoint

4

Presidential Accountability Is Decaying

Amy Davidson Sorkin

"[The president] has no conception of where he ends and the country begins."

In the following viewpoint, Amy Davidson Sorkin analyzes key points regarding the first impeachment of President Donald Trump. The author contends that Trump insisted that people do him "a favor" and seemed to confuse personal issues with official matters of the presidency, putting himself above his country. Amy Davidson Sorkin is a staff writer for the *New Yorker*. She focuses on issues of international reporting and national security.

AS YOU READ, CONSIDER THE FOLLOWING QUESTIONS:
1. According to the viewpoint, what is one of President Trump's favorite phrases?
2. What was Trump charged with in the first article of impeachment, as detailed by the author?
3. What was Trump charged with in the second article of impeachment, according to the author?

"Trump's Impeachment and the Degrading of Presidential Accountability," by Amy Davidson Sorkin, also published as "Doing Trump a Favor," *New Yorker*, February 10, 2020. Reprinted by permission.

The sordid truth of the impeachment trial of Donald Trump is that it will end with the Senate Majority Leader, Mitch McConnell, doing him a favor: delivering the votes, with little regard for the facts. That is sadly appropriate, because Trump's favors—the ones he covets, the ones he demands—and the terms on which he extracts them, remain the trial's most contested issue. The House managers cited Trump's statement to President Volodymyr Zelensky, of Ukraine, in their phone call on July 25, 2019—"I would like you to do us a favor though"—as the crux of a corrupt scheme. Trump's lawyers countered that he was talking not about his "personal interests" but about America's. In their trial brief, they argued that Trump "frequently uses variations of the phrase 'do us a favor,'" and cited examples. "Do me a favor," he said he'd asked Europe. "Would you buy a lot of soybeans, right now?" "Do me a favor," he said he'd asked North Korea. "You've got this missile engine testing site. . . . Can you close it up?" The lawyers could have added Trump's claim that, before choosing Alexander Acosta to be his Secretary of Labor, he'd worried that he was related to the CNN reporter Jim Acosta, so he told his staff, "Do me a favor—go back and check the family tree."

But, of course, what Trump was asking from Ukraine wasn't about soybean farmers' livelihoods, or arms control, or even genealogical information. He wanted dirt on a political opponent and was willing to hold up military aid for an ally in order to get it. Trump's core belief seems to have been that Ukraine, by receiving aid from America, incurred a debt that should be paid to him personally. That equation works only if, as Adam Schiff, the lead House manager, put it on Wednesday, "you view your interests as synonymous with the nation's interests." And Trump does. He has no conception of where he ends and the country begins.

Nor, apparently, do his lawyers, most notably Alan Dershowitz. "Every public official that I know believes that his election is in the public interest—and mostly you're right!" Dershowitz told the senators. And so, "if a President did something that he believes will help him get elected, in the public interest, that cannot be the kind of quid pro quo that results in impeachment." With that, Dershowitz provided a pseudo-intellectual scaffold for Trump's self-delusion.

President Bill Clinton addresses the nation in December 1998 after the US House of Representatives impeached him on charges of perjury and obstruction of justice.

Somewhere in there is the distorted echo of a real argument. A President should at least consider the electoral effect of what he does, not because his continued tenure is so important but because the opinions of citizens are. They are the ones who have to fight the wars and bear the burdens. Voters can be wrong, but even then they can still be helpful in discerning the public interest. That is the basis of democratic accountability. But Dershowitz was talking about manipulating the election process itself. In response, Senator Angus King, Independent of Maine, asked if a President could extort an Israeli Prime Minister into charging the President's opponent with anti-Semitism. In fact, by Dershowitz's logic, a President could not only seek foreign assistance in a campaign; he could unleash any number of investigations into his political opponents, declare spurious emergencies to prevent their parties' political gatherings, engage in surveillance, or take measures to limit access to polling stations—suppressing, rather than amplifying, voters' voices.

Dershowitz was arguing that, as Schiff said on Thursday, if the President believes that a deal is in his political interest, "then it doesn't matter how corrupt that quid pro quo is." Schiff was not exaggerating when he called this argument "a descent into constitutional madness." It may even prove more pernicious than the simple fact of Trump's acquittal—which was preordained, given the Republican majority's fealty to him—because the standard it sets for Presidential accountability is so degraded. It's easy to imagine defense teams playing a video of Dershowitz's presentation at a future impeachment trial, in an effort to exonerate another rogue President—perhaps one who has hung a portrait of Trump in the Oval Office. One thing that Republican senators might do, as they so flagrantly fail their country, is to clearly say that Dershowitz's reasons for acquittal are not theirs.

The first article of impeachment charged Trump with abuse of power in his dealings with Ukraine, and even a few Republicans, such as Senator Lamar Alexander, conceded that the managers had proved that case. (Alexander added that, nonetheless, the President's actions didn't warrant impeachment.) The case for the second article, charging Trump with obstruction of Congress for denying it witnesses and documents, was more complicated. Here, the Trump team's arguments were at least in the realm of constitutional reality, however hypocritically they were offered. The House managers couldn't quite shake the opinion held by many that they should have fought the President's defiance of their subpoenas in court, even if it took time. (Indeed, because Trump's arguments are so extreme and untenable, the House Democrats had been on a winning path in the lower courts.)

At the same time, the managers hammered home the point that the senators had the power to expose the full story by calling witnesses—which they chose, in a vote on Friday, to toss aside. In doing so, they may have set a precedent that will further limit future Senates in constraining Presidents. The managers also

FAST FACT

Senator Mitt Romney of Utah was the only Republican senator who voted to convict President Donald Trump of impeachment charges on Article I: Abuse of Power.

made it abundantly clear that this President has played petty games with momentous matters of war and peace.

Unable to exonerate Trump, his lawyers resorted to making an appeal to blind triumphalism. Eric Herschmann, one of the members of Trump's team most prone to go off on political tangents—he used up a lot of time attacking President Obama—reeled off a series of economic statistics and approval ratings and told the senators, "If all that is solely, solely, in their words, for his personal and political gain, and not in the best interest of the American people, then I say, God bless him. Keep doing it!" It was as if those figures added up to a paid-in-full purchase of impunity. Trump, for his part, will undoubtedly see an acquittal as further license for abuse.

Earlier in the week, Trump had held a rally in Wildwood, New Jersey, expressly to thank the now Republican congressman Jeff Van Drew for having left the Democratic Party over what Trump called the "impeachment hoax." He exhorted the crowd to reëlect Van Drew— "really a brave man, what he did was incredible"—and to throw out the Democratic "clowns." Perhaps the Republican senators, as they trudged toward casting their vote, were making a calculation about how Trump might return the favor with one for them, or their party, or their country. Or maybe they, too, can no longer tell the difference.

EVALUATING THE AUTHOR'S ARGUMENTS:

In this viewpoint, author Amy Davidson Sorkin contends that the US Senate, at the time of Trump's impeachment, took actions that might be problematic in the case of future presidential impeachments. Do you agree or disagree? Use facts from this viewpoint and previous viewpoints to back up your opinion.

Removal from Office Is Not the Only Purpose of Impeachment

"The Founders explained that impeachment was intended to have many important purposes, not just removing a president from office."

Clark D. Cunningham

In the following viewpoint, Clark D. Cunningham analyzes the thoughts and opinions of America's Founding Fathers as they struggled with setting up the Constitution and government. Cunningham details how debate occurred between individuals at the Constitutional Convention and what was decided on the issue of keeping a president in check or impeachment. Cunningham provides interesting primary source quotes, allowing a peek into the workings of the US Constitution. Clark D. Cunningham is a member of the State Bar of Georgia and directs the National Institute for Teaching Ethics & Professionalism at Georgia State University.

As Congress considers formal charges of impeachment against President Donald Trump, they should consider words spoken at the Constitutional Convention, when the Founders explained that impeachment was intended to have many important purposes, not just removing a president from office.

A critical debate took place on July 20, 1787, which resulted in adding the impeachment clause to the US Constitution. Benjamin Franklin, the oldest and probably wisest delegate at the Convention, said that when the president falls under suspicion, a "regular and peaceable inquiry" is needed.

In my work as a law professor studying original texts about the US Constitution, I've found statements made at the Constitutional Convention explaining that the Founders viewed impeachment as a regular practice with three purposes:

- To remind both the country and the president that he is not above the law
- To deter abuses of power
- To provide a fair and reliable method to resolve suspicions about misconduct.

The Convention delegates repeatedly agreed with the assertion by George Mason of Virginia, that "no point is of more importance … than the right of impeachment" because no one is "above justice."

Need for Deterrence

One of the Founders' greatest fears was that the president would abuse his power. George Mason described the president as the "man who can commit the most extensive injustice." James Madison thought the president might "pervert his administration into a scheme of [stealing public funds] or oppression or betray his trust to foreign powers." Edmund Randolph, governor of Virginia, said the president "will have great opportunitys of abusing his power; particularly in time of war when the military force, and in some respects the public money will be in his hands."

Gouverneur Morris of Pennsylvania worried that the president "may be bribed by a greater interest to betray his trust and no one would say that we ought to expose ourselves to the danger of seeing [him] in foreign pay." James Madison, himself a future president, said that in the case of the president, "corruption was within the compass of probable events … and might be fatal to the Republic."

William Davie of North Carolina argued that impeachment was "an essential security for the good behaviour" of the president; otherwise, "he will spare no efforts or means whatever to get himself re-elected." Elbridge Gerry of Massachusetts pointed out that a good president will not worry about impeachment, but a "bad one ought to be kept in fear."

Creating a Powerful Oversight Procedure

Until the very last week of the Convention, the Founders' design was for the impeachment process to start in the House of Representatives and conclude with trial in the Supreme Court.

It was not until Sept. 8, 1787, that the Convention voted to give the Senate instead the power to conduct impeachment trials.

This is clear evidence that the Convention at first wanted to combine the authority and resources of the House of Representatives to conduct the impeachment investigation—a body they called "the grand Inquest of this Nation"—with the fairness and power exemplified by trial in a court.

Even though trial of impeachments was moved from the Supreme Court to the Senate, Congress can still draw on the example of court procedures to accomplish an effective inquiry, especially if they are trying to get information from uncooperative subjects. In many of the investigations that are now part of the House's impeachment inquiry, the Trump administration has refused to hand over documents and blocked officials from testifying to Congress.

As the walls closed in around President Richard Nixon and his support in Congress dwindled, he chose to resign from office rather than wait for an impeachment vote.

The Constitution makes clear that impeachment is not a criminal prosecution: "Judgment in cases of impeachment shall not extend further than to removal from office." If impeachment trials had remained at the Supreme Court, the Court could therefore have consulted the rules it has approved for civil cases.

It makes sense that when the Convention at the last minute decided Congress would have complete power over impeachment, the delegates intended Congress would have at least the same powers the Supreme Court would have exercised.

When Courts Are Stonewalled

In civil cases, courts have powerful tools for dealing with someone who blocks access to the very information needed to judge the allegations against him.

The most commonly known method is the rule that says that once a person is legally served with a lawsuit against them, they must respond to the complaint. If they don't, the court can enter a judgment against them based on the allegations in the complaint. But there are other processes as well.

One court tool that could easily be adapted to the impeachment process comes from the federal rules of civil procedure. In a process called "request for admission," one party to a lawsuit can give their opponents a list of detailed factual allegations with a demand for a response.

If the party does not respond, the court can treat each allegation as if it were true, and proceed accordingly. If the respondent denies one or more particular allegations, there is a follow-up procedure called a request for production, demanding any documents in their possession or control supporting the denial. If the respondent refuses, again the court has the power to order that the alleged fact be taken as true.

Getting to the Truth

In an impeachment process against President Donald Trump, the House of Representatives could present the president with a request for admission to the following two simple factual statements, which could be inferred from a whistleblower complaint:

1. "In July 2019 President Trump personally issued instructions to suspend all US security assistance to Ukraine."
2. "President Trump issued these instructions with the intent to pressure the government of Ukraine to conduct a formal investigation of Hunter Biden and his father Joe Biden."

The House could give Trump a brief amount of time to respond, including providing any evidence that might disprove the allegations.

If he refused to respond, or if he denied but refused to produce supporting documentation, the House could assume the set of alleged facts to be true and include them in articles of impeachment. Then the House could vote and, depending on the outcome of that vote, the matter would then proceed to the Senate for trial.

Congress could engage in a long, drawn-out battle trying to use its oversight and subpoena powers to force various executive branch officials to release documents or testify about what they saw, heard and did. Or they could try this simple and quick procedure, which does not require the cooperation of the Department of Justice or court action.

Good for the President and the Country

One of the Dutch leaders, William V, the Prince of Orange, was suspected to have secretly sabotaged a critical alliance with France. The Dutch had no impeachment process and thus no way to conduct "a regular examination" of these allegations. These suspicions mounted, giving rise to "to the most violent animosities & contentions."

The moral to Franklin's story? If Prince William had "been impeachable, a regular & peaceable inquiry would have taken place." The prince would, "if guilty, have been duly punished—if innocent, restored to the confidence of the public."

Franklin concluded that impeachment was a process that could be "favorable" to the president, saying it is the best way to provide for "the regular punishment of the Executive when his misconduct should deserve it and for his honorable acquittal when he should be unjustly accused."

EVALUATING THE AUTHOR'S ARGUMENTS:

In this viewpoint, author Clark D. Cunningham provides readers with interesting insights into the development of the process of impeachment in the US government. Give two examples from the viewpoint article that surprise you, or that you question.

Impeachment Doesn't Need a Crime

Stefanie Lindquist

"Hamilton made no mention of the requirement that actual crimes be committed."

In the following viewpoint, Stefanie Lindquist analyzes an important point about impeachment: whether the Constitutional framers were intent to punish an individual only if crimes were committed against the United States. The author dives into the state of mind of the framers at the Constitutional Convention and the meaning they tried to convey in the Constitution when it came to impeachment. She concludes that their beliefs do not coincide with modern interpretations. Stefanie Lindquist is a professor of law at Arizona State University.

AS YOU READ, CONSIDER THE FOLLOWING QUESTIONS:
1. According to the author, what law did the president break when withholding aid to Ukraine?
2. As detailed by Lindquist, does impeachment require that crimes be committed by the impeached?
3. Did President Donald Trump commit treason, according to the viewpoint?

"Does Impeachment Need a Crime? Not According to Framers of the Constitution," by Stefanie Lindquist, The Conversation Media Group Ltd., January 26, 2020. https://theconversation.com/does-impeachment -need-a-crime-not-according-to-framers-of-the-constitution-130354. Licensed under CC BY-ND 4.0.

D onald Trump's legal and political defenders are all singing the same refrain: The president can't be impeached; he hasn't committed a crime.

Alan Dershowitz, the constitutional lawyer now representing Trump, said it during an appearance on CNN. Sen. Ted Cruz echoed it on Twitter, noting there was "not even a speeding ticket." And, of course, Trump himself has used the phrase "no crime" repeatedly as he seeks to delegitimize the impeachment hearings.

But does the impeachment and conviction of a president require an actual criminal offense, as the president's counselors and supporters argue?

Democrats clearly don't think so. Jerrold Nadler, the Democratic chair of the House Judiciary Committee, lectured senators at the impeachment hearing on Jan. 23 that the Constitution made it clear that a crime was not necessary for the president to be impeached.

This question of constitutional interpretation is critical to experts such as me, since the two articles of impeachment now pending in the Senate allege actions—including the abuse of power and the obstruction of Congress—that do not themselves constitute a violation of any criminal law.

And even though the Government Accountability Office has concluded that the President's withholding of aid to Ukraine was unlawful under the Impoundment Control Act, the president's actions do not give rise to criminal penalties.

Treason, a Matter of Dates

It's important to understand what is not on the table.

Under the impeachment clause of the Constitution, a president may be removed from office "on impeachment for, and conviction of, treason, bribery, or other high crimes and misdemeanors."

Treason is a criminal offense, defined in the Constitution as acts that "consist of levying war" against the United States or giving "aid and comfort" to its enemies. The Supreme Court has held that it can take place only in wartime.

Under this definition, Trump did not commit treason. Treason is not a catch-all phrase for unpatriotic acts. It requires actions like those of Benedict Arnold, the American general who betrayed his

President Donald J. Trump's first impeachment made headlines around the world.

country to fight for the British in the Revolutionary War. Bribery, also a criminal offense, was not alleged in the pending articles of impeachment.

Framers' Intent

That leaves us with "other high crimes and misdemeanors."

The Republican Party has long advocated for constitutional interpretation that relies on the original intent of the framers. So what did the framers mean by this lofty phrase, and what did they reject as impeachable offenses?

During the Constitutional Convention, George Mason moved that the impeachment clause follow the term "bribery" with "or maladministration."

But James Madison objected on grounds that it was too broad and would subject a president to tenure only at the pleasure of the Senate. So the phrase was replaced by "other high crimes and misdemeanors."

The framers intended the phrase to convey a more serious connotation than simple incompetence or poor administration. In Federalist Paper No. 65, Hamilton made clear that impeachable acts must involve "the abuse or violation of some public trust" and "relate chiefly to injuries done immediately to the society itself."

Hamilton made no mention of the requirement that actual crimes be committed, nor as far as I know did any other framer suggest that actual crimes were mandatory for impeachment.

Examples of impeachable offenses cited by the framers provide further context. In response to con-

cerns that the president could use his pardon powers to protect his own bad acts from detection, Madison responded: "if the president be connected, in any suspicious manner, with any person, and there be grounds to believe he will shelter him, the House of Representatives can impeach him."

Madison makes no reference to any crime. His concern here is the potential for the use of presidential power for personal or other inappropriate purposes.

Fellow framer James Iredell concluded that presidential acts to obscure or withhold information from Congress could also constitute a violation of the impeachment clause if Congress was induced to act based on the deception.

"Misdemeanors" Misinterpreted?

The framers understood that "high crimes and misdemeanors" included acts that may not necessarily violate any criminal law, but do constitute a serious violation of the public trust.

It also has to be remembered that the word "misdemeanors" had a broader meaning at the time it was added to the impeachment clause. As law professor and historian Frank Bowman has pointed out, in the context of British law at the time "misdemeanor" did not solely mean a less serious criminal offense. Rather, "crimes and misdemeanors" was used more colloquially to mean bad behavior.

Advocates for Trump say the current articles of impeachment do not meet the threshold as they do not allege criminal offenses. The framers would be surprised by this interpretation.

Originalism Revisited

The articles allege that Trump abused his political power to serve his own ends, including his reelection, and that in so doing he undermined the nation's security policy in terms of its commitment to Ukraine's defense.

Whether or not the evidence supports this charge, an actual criminal offense is simply not a prerequisite for impeachment in this or any other case. The framers are clear on this point.

Interpreting "high crimes and misdemeanors" to reflect the modern understanding of those terms as actual statutory offenses is inconsistent with the framers' original intent. Such an approach is also inconsistent with the broader theory of originalism, which relies on interpreting what the founders meant at the time of the Constitution's writing. Indeed, the president's position on "high crimes and misdemeanors" appears more consistent with the idea that the Constitution should be interpreted within a modern context as a "living" constitution—an interpretative method much criticized by many in the GOP.

EVALUATING THE AUTHOR'S ARGUMENTS:

In this viewpoint, Stefanie Lindquist argues that "high crimes and misdemeanors," while not in violation of criminal law, constitutes a serious violation of the public trust. Assuming this stance, what actions do you think constitute a violation of "high crimes and misdemeanors"?

Chapter 2

Does Impeachment Lead to Chaos?

Right or wrong, impeachment has a lasting effect on the American people.

Viewpoint

1

A Palace Crisis Is Not the Same as a Country Crisis

"Even today, if there is a crisis, it is not because government is losing credibility; it is because we have customarily attributed to government far too much credibility."

Jeffrey A. Tucker

In the following viewpoint, Jeffrey A. Tucker analyzes an important idea connected to impeachments. Does the country suffer or become embroiled in turmoil? Tucker contends that the US has not fallen into a mire because Donald Trump has been impeached. In fact, Tucker argues that it is everyday people and their communities that really hold things together in everyday life, and not the president or others in Washington, DC. Jeffrey A. Tucker is the editorial director at the American Institute for Economic Research and former director of content for the Foundation for Economic Education.

AS YOU READ, CONSIDER THE FOLLOWING QUESTIONS:

1. According to the author, who benefits from the turmoil in Washington?
2. What radical idea was put into the Constitution, according to the author?
3. As stated in the viewpoint, who is the foundation of happiness and harmony?

Technology ("Hey Google, what's the news?") and the wildly entertaining events in the Beltway have turned me into something of a news hound. Last night, I was focused on finishing up my piece on neoliberalism for several hours, during which time I had noticed the latest earth-shaking revelations from the Belly of the Beast.

The headlines were blaring yet again. Comey has a memo! He will soon tell all. Special prosecutor! I devoured these revelations. For me, this stuff has become more delightful than gaming, golfing, or pro basketball. It even bests bird watching.

The media that Trump has been demonizing since early in the campaign is loving every minute. They too are businesses and need public interest that translates to traffic and advertiser dollars. It's how they stay in business, and good for them. Trump, despite every intention, has given the "mainstream media" a second and third life. They have been hoping for a new Watergate for forty-plus years. It's their template for success, respect, and profits.

What Crisis?

But beware of one line about the unfolding soap opera in D.C.: the claim that the country is in crisis. Just this morning I read that the nation is becoming "incapacitated and paralyzed" and because its center is "tumbling toward entropy." *Vanity Fair* speaks of the "demise of the American experiment."

Don't believe it. A palace crisis is not the same thing as a country crisis. Your interest in this topic—if you are interested—is not the same as the country's interest. And truly, it turns out that most

Does Impeachment Lead to Chaos?   49

Do Americans respond to the theater of politics, or is too much emphasis put on government?

people are not paying much attention, and for good reason. They long ago wrote off national politics and White House shenanigans as not worth their attention.

My mom is a solid example. Before I was born, she was a Goldwater girl. Something happened between then and now to cause her to lose all interest. It might have been Watergate actually. It took up too many evenings. Nixon eventually resigned and Ford took over and he was eventually replaced by Carter and then Reagan and life unfolded rather normally thereafter.

After too much watching of endless Watergate hearings, and realizing that her interest didn't matter in the slightest, she became non-political, which is to say that she carried around a general hope to be left alone by all these causes, people, and political affairs. She is far more concerned about normal things: friends, home, family, and so on.

I'm not sure for whom she voted this time around. She realizes that politics is mostly theater, and there is no reason to watch if it is not what you enjoy. She certainly has no civic obligation to care about that which she cannot control.

In any case, she called me last night. I immediately started in on the latest news. I finished breathlessly and she said was glad because it gave her the chance to talk to me about why she called in the first place, which had nothing to do with all this nonsense. So far as she is concerned, there is no crisis in the land. There is only some kind of silliness happening in Washington. She's been there, done that, and won't do it again.

She intuits what many people in the media do not want to admit. The president is not what keeps the country together, if it is or ever was "together" in the way the civics texts say it should be. Not even the government generally is the reason our lives work well. For the most part, society works around government, not because of it.

The Beat Goes On

The media proclaims a crisis of democracy. But I look out the window and I see most everyone going about normal life, headed to work, school, shopping, and picking up their favorite snack from the fast food window. Admit it: nothing has really changed. And nothing will change, no matter how this mess is resolved. For most everyone who cares, D.C. antics are just solid entertainment. After all, this is why Trump is president. He engaged our interest more than his competitors.

As with Obama before him, Trump's most dedicated supporters during the election had wildly overblown expectations for the glorious things this "God Emperor" will do for the nation and world. As with Obama before him, he was glad to puff up those expectations as high as they could go. Now is the time of their demoralization. It appears that this administration will be mired in palace intrigue for a very long time, so that neither nirvana nor apocalypse will happen anytime soon.

But you would never know this from the wild panic you read in the press these days. You would swear that if someone doesn't do something drastic and fast, all systems will fail. And truly, if your worldview is such that you believe government is the reason for all life goodness and the force behind civilization itself—and the so-called "leader of the free world" is the reason for it—then you probably might panic. The center is no longer holding!

If you accept a more realistic view, it is a different matter. An example of this would be the framers themselves. They were part of a generation that literally overthrew government control, not just one part of it but the whole of it, with no plan for what might happen after. They said: down with the tyrant, and that was the end of the story.

The government they put together after the American Revolution was hardly a government at all, and it served them well for a peaceful and prosperous decade before the Constitution was ratified.

The Power to Impeach

After which the US installed a Constitution, which included something rather radical: the power to impeach the president. This power belonged to the legislature, which is to say to the representatives of the states and the people. Alexander Hamilton said at the time that the impeachment power was crucial to distinguishing our system from a monarchy.

> *The President of the United States would be liable to be impeached, tried, and, upon conviction of treason, bribery, or other high crimes or misdemeanors, removed from office; and would afterwards be liable to prosecution and punishment in the ordinary course of law. The person of the king of Great Britain [in contrast] is sacred and inviolable; there is no constitutional tribunal to which he is amenable; no punishment to which he can be subjected without involving the crisis of a national revolution. In this delicate and important circumstance of personal responsibility, the President of Confederated America would stand upon no better ground than a governor of New York, and upon worse ground than the governors of Maryland and Delaware."*
>
> *—Alexander Hamilton, Federalist 69*

Now, if the framers believed that the president was so crucial to life functioning, they wouldn't have made it possible for the legislature to constantly threaten the person with losing his job. You get the sense from reading the Federalist Papers that they expected that impeachment would happen fairly regularly and be threatened constantly. This was never true under monarchy (unless a portion of the public disbelieved that the correct sovereign was in power).

True, the powers of the presidency were far fewer in those days but this too should be a wake-up call to people left, right, and center. If the threat of impeachment really is that destabilizing to life itself, it is probably the case that the presidency needs radically to have its power and authority reduced.

Even today, if there is a crisis, it is not because government is losing credibility; it is because we have customarily attributed to government far too much credibility.

The Markets

Now, part of the cited evidence for why this D.C. drama is more than entertainment concerns the financial markets. They have been under pressure at home and abroad ever since the revelations of all sorts of White House perfidy. Why is this? Most likely, the prices of financial assets have soared since Trump's election due to the expectation of tax and regulatory cuts. A crippled presidency and Republican party make those far less likely.

For me, this is very sad. Call me naive, but I actually believed that this might be one source of good to come from this administration, amidst much rightly denounced bad. I even hoped for health care reform. These are not to be, not any time soon. We are once again back to confusion, distraction, and inaction in government.

I can think of worse fates. Some very bad ideas—trade wars, drug wars, the rebuilding of the prison state, trillion-dollar infrastructure, and so on—might also be stopped.

Perhaps this is a good time to regroup, reset, rethink. For anyone who depends on a finely tuned policy and governing apparatus to be the reason for the good life, it might be time to prepare for a new way of thinking and living.

Which might be a silver lining to emerge from this political season. If the D.C. intrigue inspires the American people to prepare for life without help from Washington, it might all be worth it.

Trump once said that the nation-state "remains the true foundation for happiness and harmony." Not really. It's just you, me, our friends and family, our communities, our trading relationships, and so on. It's just us. And that's a great thing to realize.

EVALUATING THE AUTHOR'S ARGUMENTS:

Viewpoint author Jeffrey A. Tucker suggests that the president is not ultimately in control of the happiness and harmony in the United States. Do you agree or disagree? Use examples from the article and your personal life to support your opinion.

Viewpoint
2

President Trump's Impeachment Was Drama, Not Chaos

"Trump has told allies and friends that he wanted a splashy Senate trial with high-profile attorneys and witnesses."

Nancy Cook

In the following viewpoint, Nancy Cook reports on the proceedings of President Donald Trump's impeachment. Cook details the workings in the White House, the main players in the action, and some of the strategies used to help Trump in the quest to be acquitted from impeachment. Cook reviews strategies offered and used by White House people, but in the end, she points out that Trump is calling the shots. Nancy Cook is a White House reporter for Politico.

AS YOU READ, CONSIDER THE FOLLOWING QUESTIONS:

1. Who is the chief impeachment strategist, according to the viewpoint?
2. Which impeachment in history was studied by White House personnel to guide this impeachment?
3. According to the author, who is really running everything with the impeachment proceedings?

"Trump's Impeachment Chaos Evolves into a White House Strategy," by Nancy Cook, December 16, 2019. Reprinted by permission of Politico SPRL. Copyright 2016 Politico LLC.

The White House's chaotic infighting over its impeachment strategy has mostly subsided, replaced by casting and choreography decisions designed to guide the US president through a quick trial with the least drama possible.

It's a sharp shift from the widespread confusion and constant jockeying for influence that dominated the early march toward impeachment this fall. Now, White House officials have settled into specific roles just in time to roll from an expected House impeachment vote this week to a Senate trial in January.

Apart from US President Donald Trump, the chief impeachment strategist is Pat Cipollone, the White House's top attorney. During his one year in the position, he's managed to maintain an excellent relationship with the president—unlike his predecessor, Don McGahn—and has morphed into the primary architect of the White House strategy, so much so that he is expected to act as the lead counsel during the Senate proceedings.

"The White House counsel is playing the lead role because of the nature of all of it and the two articles of impeachment," said a person familiar with the White House planning. "It only makes sense because he needs to defend the institution of the presidency."

While the full House of Representatives is waiting to vote on the two articles of impeachment as early as Wednesday, the attention of top White House aides has already shifted to the Senate trial. Both Trump and his aides predict a more favorable process in the Republican-controlled chamber.

"At this point, the House process is what it is," a senior administration official said. "We've answered all of the House letters. The Senate trial has definitely become the focus."

That Senate trial gives White House aides the opportunity to show the president they can work in lockstep and not become consumed by the frequent tripwires of working in the West Wing, including constant machinations over personnel and power grabs.

Both White House and Senate aides have been closely studying the impeachment trial of President Bill Clinton as an example of how to model this Senate trial, even if the charges against the two presidents remain wildly different. Clinton faced impeachment for lying about his sexual relationship with a White House intern, while

The Senate chamber at the US Capitol is where impeachment trials take place.

Trump embroiled himself in his own impeachment scandal by asking a foreign leader to investigate a political rival ahead of his 2020 reelection campaign.

Senate leadership still needs to set the exact parameters, rules and length of the trial, though people familiar with the planning say the trial likely will not include any witnesses. If that is the case, the Senate trial would kick off with opening arguments before each side would make their case.

"We did nothing wrong. So, I'll do long, or short. I've heard Mitch. I've heard Lindsey. I think they are very much in agreement on some concept," Trump said Friday, referring to Senate Majority Leader Mitch McConnell and top Senate ally Lindsey Graham, when asked about the structure and length of a Senate trial. "I'll do whatever they want to do. It doesn't matter. I wouldn't mind the long process, because I'd like to see the whistleblower, who's a fraud."

In recent weeks, Trump has told allies and friends that he wanted a splashy Senate trial with high-profile attorneys and witnesses such as Hunter Biden, son of Democratic candidate and former Vice President Joe Biden.

But McConnell has been urging Trump to instead settle on a short trial; brevity allows the Senate greater control over the narrative without the unpredictability witness testimony can bring.

"Look, it is the US Senate. It will never be that flashy," said a Republican close to the White House.

In recent weeks, Cipollone has made several trips to Capitol Hill to meet with Republican senators over lunch, or with McConnell to chart the impeachment strategy. He also frequently speaks with the group of senators who also are lawyers such as Utah Senator Mike Lee, who once clerked for Alito when he served on the 3rd US Circuit Court of Appeals.

Aiding Cipollone's outreach to Capitol Hill is the White House director of legislative affairs, Eric Ueland, a longtime veteran of Senate leadership and the former staff director of the Senate Budget Committee who's known for his mastery of arcane Senate rules and procedures.

"The White House is lucky to have somebody who has a very good, experienced track record, and memory for a number of fights which seemed obscure at the time but that now have become relevant," said Dave Hoppe, chief of staff to former Senate Majority Leader Trent Lott.

"Eric was a senior staffer among Republican leadership staff when we were doing impeachment 21 years ago."

During the Clinton impeachment, Ueland served as a senior staffer to Senator Don Nickles, who at the time was the second-ranking Republican in the Senate, and was part of a tiny group of staffers allowed to sit and work on the Senate floor, giving access to the country's last impeachment trial.

"He has seen it done before," Hoppe said even if the players and charges are now different.

Acting White House chief of staff Mick Mulvaney remains involved in the impeachment proceedings and attends impeachment meetings, even if Cipollone is taking the lead among staff on strategy. One senior administration official described Mulvaney's role as convening allies and aides when needed, such as bringing lawmakers to Camp David in recent months in an effort to keep the Republican Party unified.

Jared Kushner, as one of the president's most trusted aides, remains involved in impeachment when needed, according to two senior administration officials, alongside with his work in negotiating the US-Mexico-Canada trade deal, China trade deal, Middle East plan and running the 2020 campaign.

As the White House press secretary and communications director, Stephanie Grisham is overseeing the communications effort. She's being helped temporarily by Pam Bondi, the former Florida attorney general, and Tony Sayegh, a former top Treasury official and ally of Secretary Steven Mnuchin.

Both Bondi and Sayegh have visited Capitol Hill several times in recent weeks to meet with Senate and House communicators to keep the White House and congressional messages in sync.

Even as White House officials find their spots in the impeachment lineup, several current and former administration officials cautioned that Trump as always remains the one to dictate the message and ideas.

"Everyone has resigned themselves to the idea that the president is always running everything," said a former senior administration official.

EVALUATING THE AUTHOR'S ARGUMENTS:

Viewpoint author Nancy Cook reports that President Donald Trump's impeachment became a strategy instead of chaos. Do you agree or disagree with this analysis? Support your view with details from the viewpoint.

Impeachment Outcomes Depend on Party Support

"The overwhelming majority of Republican politicians are either supporting him or remaining silent."

Dennis Altman

In the following viewpoint, Dennis Altman maintains that the impeachment proceedings against President Donald Trump, while not causing chaos, surely are a cause for concern for both Republicans and Democrats. Altman provides details about Trump's first impeachment while comparing it to historical dramas and drawing interesting comparisons to one US senator in particular. Finally, Altman analyzes a few of the Democratic candidates trying to unseat President Trump. Dennis Altman is a professorial fellow at LaTrobe University.

AS YOU READ, CONSIDER THE FOLLOWING QUESTIONS:

1. Which two senators claimed Trump to be unfit for the presidency, according to the viewpoint?
2. What happened with Senator Joe McCarthy, as reported by the author?
3. What happened to Richard Nixon, as stated in the viewpoint?

"How the Impeachment Inquiry Might Affect Trump's 2020 Re-Election Chances," by Dennis Altman, The Conversation, October 3, 2019. https://theconversation.com/how-the-impeachment-inquiry-might-affect -trumps-2020-re-election-chances-124424. Licensed under CC BY-ND 4.0.

Many Republicans in Congress felt they had to show support for Donald Trump during his impeachment proceedings for fear of losing their upcoming elections.

T he next 13 months will see American politics completely dominated by the fate of Donald Trump. As the House of Representatives moves towards impeaching him, leading to a hearing which then moves to the Senate, the Democrats will be engaged in an increasingly bitter contest for the nomination to run against Trump in the November 2020 elections.

At this stage, it appears there are the numbers in the House for impeachment, which entails formally charging the president with "high crimes and misdemeanors." Their indictment then moves to the Senate, which can remove the president by a two-thirds majority, in a hearing chaired by the chief justice.

Because 2020 is an election year, both sides will manage proceedings with an eye to the November poll. It is possible the House will vote before the end of the year: the decision to impeach Bill Clinton for lying under oath was made in the last three months of 1998.

Clinton was cleared by the Senate by the following February, so it is also possible the Senate will hold its own proceedings before most of the presidential primaries commence. It takes two-thirds of the Senate to remove a president from office, which has never happened.

While several Republican House representatives have expressed concern about the president's behaviour, the overwhelming majority of Republican politicians are either supporting him or remaining silent.

Rather as Boris Johnson seems to have captured the British Conservative Party, so Trump has imposed himself on the Republicans. Those who three years ago assailed his unfitness for the presidency, such as Lindsey Graham and Ted Cruz, are now his loudest defenders. Meanwhile, several of his opponents are withdrawing from political office.

However, Senator Mitt Romney, Republican candidate for president in 2012, has indicated his disquiet, which is almost certainly shared by others. If the House uncovers more apparently illegal activity on Trump, and if public opinion seems to be turning against the president, there are several other senators who may follow, if only to preserve their own positions. Republican senators are facing re-election in states such as Colorado, Iowa, Maine and North Carolina, where they are increasingly vulnerable.

There is an odd historical parallel with the history of Senator Joe McCarthy, who led increasingly virulent anti-Communist crusades in the early 1950s and whose protégé, Roy Cohn, in turn influenced Trump.

Eventually, Republican senators turned on McCarthy, and censured but did not expel him. But this happened only once it was clear that public support for McCarthy was collapsing, which is so far not evident for Trump.

Faced with possible impeachment and loss of support, Richard Nixon resigned. It is difficult to see Trump doing this—it is more likely he will become even more irrational and vengeful as the process winds on. Right-wing media will echo the president's claim that the impeachment hearings represent treason, with real danger of violent clashes between supporters and opponents of Trump.

For the Democrats, the best outcome would be a split within Republican ranks, which leaves Trump in office but weakened and vulnerable to a challenge for re-nomination. Removing Trump would place Vice President Mike Pence in office, and presumably ensured of nomination in 2020.

The dilemma for the Democrats is that the impeachment process will dominate the news cycle as they jockey for position going into next year's long battle for the presidential nomination. Trump will use the allegations to focus attention on former Vice President Joe Biden, whose son's business dealings in Ukraine triggered the impeachment inquiry.

Biden may hope this will allow him to emerge as the injured defender of political propriety, but he will be tarnished through guilt by association, and is likely to slip further in the polls. Biden represents some of the traditional working class and African American base of the Democratic Party, and how they react could determine the ultimate Democrat candidate.

At the moment, Elizabeth Warren challenges Biden's lead in the polls, with Bernie Sanders the only other candidate consistently supported by more than 10% of Democrats. None of the others in a crowded field—12 have qualified to take part in the next televised Democratic debate—have much support, and they will start to drop out once the primary season begins in February 2020.

If Biden continues to lose support, there is room for someone to emerge as the moderate front-runner, given that both Warren and Sanders represent the more radical instincts of the party. This is presumably why so many candidates are determined to continue campaigning, even when some of them rarely muster 2% in the polls.

Were Sanders' current health problems to lead to his withdrawal most of his support would presumably switch to Warren. Predictions are risky, and my record is poor. But it is increasingly likely that the Democrats will nominate someone other than an old white man in 2020, betting on a figure like Barack Obama who can galvanise a bitterly divided nation and persuade people to turn out and vote.

Presidential Impeachment Is Not Necessarily a Coup

"For some in the Latin American left, anything that cuts short a president's tenure in office...is a coup."

Juan Carlos Hidalgo

In the following viewpoint, Juan Carlos Hidalgo details a recent impeachment that took place in Brazil. Hidalgo analyzes and debunks common misperceptions regarding the impeachment process in general, and specifically how it relates to the 2016 impeachment of Brazilian president Dilma Rousseff. Juan Carlos Hidalgo is a policy analyst at the Center for Global Liberty and Prosperity focusing on Latin America.

AS YOU READ, CONSIDER THE FOLLOWING QUESTIONS:
1. Where is Brazil's impeachment process outlined, as detailed by the viewpoint?
2. According to the author, why was Brazil's president impeached?
3. According to the viewpoint, how is Brazil's media viewed differently than President Trump's view of the US media?

During the Trump administration, House Speaker Nancy Pelosi (far left) and Senate Minority Leader Chuck Schumer (second from right) were often at odds with Senate Majority Leader Mitch McConnell (third from right).

O n Sunday night, Brazil's Chamber of Deputies voted overwhelmingly (367-137) to open impeachment proceedings
against President Dilma Rousseff. The Senate will now
vote on whether to take the case and try her, which is all but guar-
anteed. As a matter of fact, barring some unforeseen event, Dilma's
days as president are numbered.

These are Brazil's most turbulent months since the return to
democracy in 1985. Not only is the president about to be removed
from office, but the country is also mired in its worst economic reces-
sion since the 1930s. It is not coincidence that Dilma's popularity
(10%) stands at a similar level to Brazil's fiscal deficit (10.75%), the
unemployment rate (9.5%), and the inflation rate (9.4%). The economic and political crises are feeding off of one another.

Here are some facts and myths regarding this impeachment
process:

1. "It's a Coup!"

For some in the Latin American left, anything that cuts short a president's tenure in office—even if it's an impeachment process stipulated in the Constitution—is a coup. The same narrative was applied when left-wing President Fernando Lugo was impeached by Paraguay's Congress in 2012.

The impeachment process and the crimes for which a president can be impeached in Brazil are clearly outlined in articles 85 and 86 of the Constitution. Moreover, the entire process has been overseen by the Supreme Court, which has thus far found no fault in how things have been conducted. It's important to add that 8 of the 11 justices in the Supreme Court were appointed by Dilma and her Workers' Party predecessor, Lula da Silva.

Tellingly, when the Guatemalan Congress voted last year to strip right-wing President Otto Pérez Molina of his immunity, so he could be prosecuted for corruption charges, no one claimed it was a coup.

2. "Dilma Hasn't Been Accused of Any Wrongdoing"

It is true that Dilma hasn't been accused of personally being involved in the Petrobras bribing scheme that inflicted loses of $17 billion on the state-owned oil company. Even though she was the chairwoman of the oil giant when most of the corrupt deals took place, her defense is that she was unaware that this was going on; at any rate, not a very good show of competence.

However, President Rousseff is not being impeached over the Petrobras corruption scandal, but over her government's illegal handling of budgetary accounts. In this regard, it was an independent court—the Federal Accounts Court—that ruled that the Rousseff administration had broken the law. According to article 85 of Brazil's Constitution, this is a crime for which a president can be impeached.

3. "Most of the Members of Congress Are Implicated in Corruption Scandals"

This is actually true. According to an NGO called Transparência Brasil, 60% of members of Congress have been convicted or are under investigation for various crimes, including corruption and electoral fraud. The speaker of the Chamber of Deputies, Eduardo Cunha, has been charged with taking millions of dollars in bribes under the Petrobras scheme.

It is true that Brazilians aren't simply dealing with a corrupt ruling party, but a crooked political class. Impeachment won't fix this, but it will certainly set a powerful precedent. However, if the ultimate aim of Brazilians is to clean up the political system, they must be more rigorous in how they elect their political leaders in the future.

Other reforms are badly needed, such as overhauling the rules that grant immunity to members of Congress when they face criminal charges. Brazilians who have taken to the streets demanding the ouster of Dilma should now set their sights on political reform and those who oppose it.

4. "There Is a Political Vendetta Against the Workers' Party from the Judiciary and the Right-Wing Media"

It is true that Brazil's judicial institutions, including the federal police, the attorney general's office, and leading judges have been very active uncovering, prosecuting and convicting politicians involved in corruption scandals. But those implicated thus far have belonged to different political parties, including those of the opposition. As mentioned above, the speaker of the Chamber of Deputies leading the impeachment process against Dilma has been charged with corruption.

The media has also played a critical role in exposing the Petrobras scheme. This is good. Unlike other South American countries where the press has been stifled by their governments, in Brazil there is a vibrant and free press that hold politicians accountable, and not only those that belong to the incumbent party. As a matter of fact, big news outlets considered "anti-Workers' Party" have exposed the shenanigans of Speaker Eduardo Cunha and pointed out the fact that numerous Congressmen impeaching Dilma are also facing their own corruption charges. This doesn't look like a cover-up.

The impeachment process is without a doubt a distressing affair for Brazil's young democracy. But the country will emerge stronger if the right lessons are learned.

EVALUATING THE AUTHOR'S ARGUMENTS:

Viewpoint author Juan Carlos Hidalgo makes the case that many parts of Brazil's government are infiltrated by corruption. According to the details in the viewpoint, what might help lessen the grip of corruption?

"It's a perfect time to remember what that Nixon generation learned: regardless of ideology, absolute power corrupts absolutely."

Nixon's Impeachment Ushered In the End of Trust in Government

Jeffrey A. Tucker

In the following viewpoint, Jeffrey A. Tucker analyzes a time in history when Richard Nixon was president before he was impeached and resigned from office. Tucker draws comparisons to modern times and points out how the Libertarian party in the US came to be. Tucker also points to what may be similarities to Donald Trump and the reasons why his supporters follow him seemingly with abandon. Jeffrey A. Tucker is the editorial director at the American Institute for Economic Research.

AS YOU READ, CONSIDER THE FOLLOWING QUESTIONS:

1. What made Richard Nixon a hero in his early days as a politician, according to the viewpoint?
2. How was the Libertarian Party launched by Nixon?
3. What did the Nixon generation learn about political power, according to the author?

I f you have followed the Republican trajectory over the last year, perhaps this will not surprise you. And maybe you discerned this last week when "Law and Order" became another official Republican campaign slogan, alongside "Make America Great Again."

As it turns out, the model that the Donald Trump campaign is using for its public image, messaging, and policies was the one pioneered by Richard Nixon in 1968. Trump's campaign manager Paul Manafort confirmed it.

Then the candidate himself agreed. "I think what Nixon understood is that when the world is falling apart, people want a strong leader whose highest priority is protecting America first," Trump said. "The '60s were bad, really bad. And it's really bad now. Americans feel like it's chaos again."

Nixon Was the Turning Point

Nixon was a remarkable case. His public credibility was built by his big role in the 1948 congressional hearings that pitted State Department Official Alger Hiss against Whittaker Chambers. Nixon was then a congressman from California and a key player on the House UnAmerican Activities Committee (HUAC). He publicly demonstrated Hiss's Communist Party connections, and thereby became a hero to the anti-communists of that time.

The event became the cornerstone of Nixon's entire career, establishing him as the leader of the anti-leftist faction of the party. Based on this reputation, he went from the House to the Senate in 1950, to the Vice Presidency in 1952, and finally the Presidency in 1968. Upon his election, hopes were high among the libertarians of the time that he would perhaps work to dismantle the welfarism and warfarism of the Lyndon Johnson era.

I recall my father telling me about his own feelings at the time. "I never trusted Nixon," he told me years later. "But we shared the same enemies. At the time, that was enough for me."

Even in those days, the Republican Party was a coalition of disparate groups: foreign policy hawks, law and order conservatives, and the libertarian-minded merchant class that was sick of government spending, inflation, taxation, and regulation. The political priorities

Some take the view that American citizens should be given the choice to vote the accused out of office rather than endure the chaos of impeachment.

of the groups were in tension, often in contradiction. Which would prevail?

As it turned out, Nixon would devastate the anti-communist crowd by opening up diplomatic relations with China. But that was nothing compared to his complete betrayal of the libertarians, who had reluctantly supported him. He began the drug war that was specifically structured to harm blacks and hippies. He ordered IRS audits of his enemies.

Nixon closed the gold window and officially put the monetary system on a paper standard—thus realizing the dreams of decades of Keynesians and backers of big government. He pushed the Fed for more inflation. He founded the Environmental Protection Agency, which has harassed private property owners ever since.

Most egregiously and shockingly, on August 15, 1971, Nixon announced to the nation a policy that hadn't been experienced since World War II. It was like a scene from *Atlas Shrugged*. "I am today ordering a freeze on all prices and wages throughout the United States," he said. After the freeze, all price increases were to be approved by a pay board and a price commission.

Galvanizing the Libertarians

This was the event that led the libertarians to gain a heightened consciousness of the task before them. What had previously been a loose association of intellectuals and a few other writers became a mass movement of students, donors, organizations, publications, and activists. The Libertarian Party was founded. *Reason Magazine*, founded as a mimeographed pamphlet in 1968, became a real magazine with an actual publication schedule. Ron Paul, under the intellectual influence of the Foundation for Economic Education, decided to enter public life.

Murray Rothbard captured the spirit of outrage that gave birth to the libertarian movement. He wrote the following in the *New York Times* on September 4, 1971:

> *On Aug. 15, 1971, fascism came to America. And everyone cheered, hailing the fact that a "strong President" was once again at the helm. The word fascism is scarcely an exaggeration to describe the New Economic Policy. The trend had been there for years, in the encroachment of Big Government over all aspects of the economy and society, in growing taxes, subsidies, and controls, and in the shift of economic decision-making from the free market to the Federal Government. The most recent ominous development was the bailout of Lockheed, which established the principle that no major corporation, no matter how inefficient, can be allowed to go under.*
>
> *But the wage-price freeze, imposed in sudden hysteria on Aug. 15, spells the end of the free price system and therefore of the entire system of free enterprise and free markets that have been the heart of the American economy. The main horror of the wage-price freeze is that this is totalitarianism and nobody seems to care...*
>
> *The worst part of our leap into fascism is that no one and no group, left, right, or center, Democrat or Republican, businessman, journalist or economic, has attacked the principle of the move itself. The unions and the Democrats are only concerned that the policy wasn't total enough, that*

it didn't cover interest and profits. The ranks of business seem to have completely forgotten all their old rhetoric about free enterprise and the free price system; indeed, the Washington Post reported that the mood of business and banks is "almost euphoric."…

The conservatives, too, seem to have forgotten their free enterprise rhetoric and are willing to join in the patriotic hoopla. The New Left and the practitioners of the New Politics seem to have forgotten all their rhetoric about the evils of central control …

It was this article, and the events he described, that made the libertarians realize that they needed their own movement, something different from the left and right, and outside the Democrats and Republicans, each of whom represent their own kind of tyranny. Never again would they trust the promises of a "strong president." Never again would they trust a mainstream party.

The experience with Nixon taught those who seek more freedom that there is a huge difference between merely hating the left and actually loving liberty. The lesson was burned into the hearts and minds of a whole generation: to see your enemies crawl before you is not really a victory. The only real victory would be freedom itself. And to love liberty is neither left nor right. Libertarianism is a third way, a worthy successor to the great liberal movement from the 17th-19th centuries, the movement that established free trade, worked for peace, celebrated prosperity through freedom, ended slavery, liberated women, and universalized human rights.

The realization marked a new era in American political life.

Then There Was Watergate

When Nixon was finally driven out of office following the Watergate scandal, conservatives wept. But the libertarians, having now developed a sense of their task quite apart from the rightest cultural and political agenda, cheered the end of the cult of the Presidency. By then, Nixon had become their bete noir.

Rothbard wrote:

It is Watergate that gives us the greatest single hope for the short-run victory of liberty in America. For Watergate, as politicians have been warning us ever since, destroyed the public's "faith in government"—and it was high time, too. Watergate engendered a radical shift in the deep-seated attitudes of everyone—regardless of their explicit ideology— toward government itself. For in the first place, Watergate awakened everyone to the invasions of personal liberty and private property by government—to its bugging, drugging, wiretapping, mail covering, agents provocateurs—even assassinations. Watergate at last desanctified our previously sacrosanct FBI and CIA and caused them to be looked at clearly and coolly.

But more important, by bringing about the impeachment of the President, Watergate permanently desanctified an office that had come to be virtually considered as sovereign by the American public. No longer will the President be considered above the law; no longer will the President be able to do no wrong. But most important of all, government itself has been largely desanctified in America. No one trusts politicians or government anymore; all government is viewed with abiding hostility, thus returning us to that state of healthy distrust of government.

It's almost a half century later and the Republicans have once again chosen a man who is loved mainly because of the people he hates and those who hate him back. And once again, we are being told that greatness, law, and order should be the goal. Once again, the right is defining itself as anti-left while the left is defining itself as anti-right, even while both favor centralist and nationalist agendas.

It's a perfect time to remember what that Nixon generation learned: regardless of ideology, absolute power corrupts absolutely. Even twenty years later, libertarians were

FAST FACT

On August 15, 1971, President Richard Nixon ordered a freeze on all wages in the United States.

highly skeptical of Ronald Reagan for this reason. It wasn't until he showed himself to be a very different kind of candidate than Nixon—Reagan was very clear that the real enemy of the American people was government itself—that libertarians went along.

Regardless of the personalities ascendent at the moment, the real struggle we face is between the voluntary associations that constitute the beautiful part of our lives, on the one hand, and, on the other, the legal monopoly of violence and compulsion by the institutions of the state, which lives at the expense of society.

If you don't like government as we know it, you need to decide why. Is it because you believe in a social order that minimizes coercion and unleashes human creativity to build peace and prosperity? Or is it because you think the wrong people are running it and we need a strong leader to put them in their place? This is the major division in politics today.

EVALUATING THE AUTHOR'S ARGUMENTS:

In this viewpoint, Jeffrey A. Tucker suggests that the Nixon presidency and consequent Watergate impeachment scandal moved people to not trust the government. Do you think people have the same feelings about the two presidents (Clinton and Trump) impeached since then? Why or why not?

Chapter 3

Should the Impeachment Process Be Changed?

Does the current process of impeachment ever lead to justice?

Viewpoint

1

"It has become difficult to imagine two-thirds of senators voting to convict a President, even for egregious abuses."

Hyper-Partisanship Has Rendered Impeachment Pointless

Michael Luo

In the following viewpoint, Michael Luo details the impeachment process and how it has functioned in the past and how it continues to serve the US in the present. Luo argues that the framers of the Constitution built safeguards into the US government through the impeachment process and demonstrates how it is still a valid and necessary option in US democracy. Michael Luo is editor for the online content of the *New Yorker*. He writes regularly on religion, media, and politics.

AS YOU READ, CONSIDER THE FOLLOWING QUESTIONS:
1. What vote in the Senate can remove a US president?
2. How could a partisan stalemate in impeachment end, according to the author?
3. What is missing from the oath that guides senators during impeachment proceedings?

The historical record reveals little about the rationale behind one of the most crucial decisions the Framers of the US Constitution made on impeachment: that two-thirds of the Senate must agree to remove the President. That requirement was a departure from the British model, in which the House of Commons brings charges and the House of Lords hears cases but only a simple majority is required for conviction. In the original Constitution, only a handful of other actions were bound to a supermajority: overriding Presidential vetoes, the approval of treaties, expelling members of Congress, and proposing constitutional amendments. In Federalist No. 58, James Madison wrote that requiring more than a majority for certain decisions can serve "as an additional shield to some particular interests, and another obstacle generally to hasty and partial measures."

The party system that today defines our politics—and its dysfunction—did not exist at the time of the Constitutional Convention but would begin to emerge in the seventeen-nineties. With just two major political parties, the biggest implication of the supermajority requirement is that impeachment must usually achieve a degree of bipartisan consensus in order to satisfy its ultimate objective—the ending of a Presidency. In his classic treatise "Congressional Government: A Study in American Politics," Woodrow Wilson described the processes that accompany impeachment as "ponderous and difficult to handle," not unlike the steps required to formally amend the Constitution. "Indignation so great as to overgrow party interest may secure a conviction," he wrote. "Nothing less can."

In retrospect, the Framers' decision to set a higher bar for conviction provided a useful measure of protection for American democracy under the two-party system. The founders had struggled over the proper calibration of the impeachment clause, wanting to insure that the language was broad enough to encompass serious violations of public trust but not so open to interpretation as to leave the process vulnerable to the whims of a determined faction. If a simple majority were all that was required for the removal of a President, it is easy to see how impeachment could become a destabilizing political weapon, wielded by losing parties to nullify election results.

With Congress divided along party lines, it seems impossible that a president would be convicted in the current political climate.

The current hyper-partisanship of American politics, however, presents the opposite danger. It has become difficult to imagine two-thirds of senators voting to convict a President, even for egregious abuses. During Watergate, congressional Republicans stuck by Richard Nixon for months, even as revelations about his Administration's involvement in the burglary and subsequent coverup accumulated in newspaper accounts and through the Senate Watergate Committee. Only after the release of the "smoking gun" recording that revealed Nixon had ordered the F.B.I. to halt its investigation into the break-in did Republican intransigence finally dissolve. Two days later, a delegation of senior Republican leaders visited the Oval Office to inform Nixon that he could no longer escape impeachment in the House and conviction in the Senate. The next day, Nixon announced his decision to resign.

At the time, talk of Presidential impeachment was relatively unusual, and it remained so after the trauma of Watergate. Since Bill Clinton's impeachment, however, it has become a standard feature of the partisan landscape. In their book "To End a Presidency: The Power of Impeachment," Laurence Tribe and Joshua Matz characterize this development as the "permanent impeachment campaign." Neither Barack Obama nor George W. Bush faced formal impeachment proceedings, but the period following the Clinton Presidency was marked by frequent demands for Presidential removal. "Impeachment had become an

accepted, predicted tool of partisan combat," Tribe and Matz write. The consequences of these unrelenting escalations are potentially difficult to discern, at least before it is too late. "A nation over-saturated with impeachment talk," they write, "may find it especially difficult to remove a president from office when it's really, truly necessary."

This aptly describes the current situation with Donald Trump. The leveraging of American foreign policy for personal political ends, as Trump appears to have done with Ukraine, certainly falls within the realm of egregious violations of public trust—precisely the kind of abuse of executive power that impeachment was designed to guard against. Democratic leaders are pushing ahead with evidence-gathering, calling witnesses, and issuing subpoenas. Each day brings new developments—on Thursday, federal prosecutors unsealed an indictment on campaign-finance violations against two men who had been enlisted by the President's personal lawyer, Rudy Giuliani, to help in the effort to obtain damaging information about the former Vice-President Joe Biden in Ukraine. But the Trump Administration has obstructed at nearly every turn, claiming Democrats are violating tenets of due process and that they are seeking to overturn the results of the 2016 election. The modern Republican Party, meanwhile, bears little resemblance to the G.O.P. of the Nixon Presidency. Moderates have all but disappeared as the Party's ideological center has lurched rightward. Trump has remade the Party in his own image, aided by a thriving right-wing media ecosystem. Disloyalty is punished; cohesion is maintained through fear.

As it stands, the most likely outcome of the Democrats' inquiry is that Trump will be impeached along party lines in the House and acquitted in the Republican-led Senate. But a failure to reach consensus on the President's misdeeds carries repercussions far beyond his Presidency and even the next election. An impeachment and acquittal, voted strictly along party lines, would send the past two decades' internecine conflict into a new, more dangerous realm. Aggrieved Republicans would be able to point to the Senate's decision to acquit and accuse Democrats of a coup attempt for partisan gain. If Republicans were able to regain control of the House but fall short of the White House, impeachment would likely be trotted back out at the earliest opportunity. It is easy to see the ratcheting of recriminations morphing into an inescapable vise of political dysfunction.

There is, however, a way out of this cycle, even if it is difficult to imagine at the present moment. Twenty Republican senators of conscience would need to lead the way and join Senate Democrats. Since House Speaker Nancy Pelosi announced the impeachment inquiry, last month, at least a half-dozen Republican senators have expressed varying levels of opprobrium of Trump. Susan Collins, of Maine, and Ben Sasse, of Nebraska, took Trump to task for his remarks from the White House lawn calling upon China to investigate the Biden family. John Thune, of South Dakota, and Rob Portman, of Ohio, chided Trump for pressuring Ukrainian leaders to investigate Biden. Of all the Republican senators, however, Mitt Romney, the former Republican Presidential nominee and now the junior senator from Utah, has been the most forceful. "By all appearances, the President's brazen and unprecedented appeal to China and to Ukraine to investigate Joe Biden is wrong and appalling," Romney said on Twitter last week. "When the only American citizen President Trump singles out for China's investigation is his political opponent in the midst of the Democratic nomination process, it strains credulity to suggest that it is anything other than politically motivated."

Romney has certainly demonstrated the capacity, in the past, to exercise moral leadership. During the 2016 campaign, he delivered an extraordinary speech denouncing Trump, who had become the Republican front-runner, as a "con man, a fake." And, on the eve of his swearing-in to the US Senate, Romney published an op-ed in the *Washington Post* that asserted that Trump "has not risen to the mantle of the office." Romney's role model in public service has long been his father, George Romney, the former Republican governor of Michigan, who was known for his abiding principles, support for civil rights, and political moderation. Romney is not up for reëlection until 2024; Trump's hold on G.O.P. voters is also weaker in Utah than it is elsewhere. But one of the conundrums of Romney's political career has been his maddening inconsistency. Political opportunism has sometimes trumped principle, such as when he courted Trump to become Secretary of State.

In the end, the outcome will rest upon the scruples of every Republican senator, weighing the evidence and considering the consequences. Should articles of impeachment reach the Senate, the proceedings will largely follow the framework set out for the first Presidential-impeachment trial, in 1868, of Andrew Johnson, who had fought bitterly with Congress over how much leniency to grant Southern states after the Civil War. Each senator will come forward to sign his or her name under an oath—the same one that senators swore to uphold a century and a half ago, for the Johnson trial, and did again during the Clinton impeachment—promising to "do impartial justice according to the Constitution and laws." Notably, in the oath, there is no mention of party.

EVALUATING THE AUTHOR'S ARGUMENTS:

Viewpoint author Michael Luo focuses attention on the fact that two-thirds of the Senate must agree in order to oust a US president. Do you believe the Founders were correct to frame the impeachment process like this? Support your opinion with details from the viewpoint.

Viewpoint

2

Questioning the Legitimacy of Impeachment Is a Distraction

"Americans are relying on their political predispositions and preferred party leaders' stances to shape their perspectives."

Kate Gundersen

In the following viewpoint, Kate Gundersen argues that the extreme polarization of political parties in the US makes it essentially impossible for an impeachment of Donald Trump to take place. Gundersen details facts that demonstrate people are too swayed by their political party affiliation and consequently are not judging the facts presented by Congress. Instead the public is just parroting their political party's line and not making intelligent decisions after weighing the evidence, hence not making up their own minds. Kate Gundersen is associate covers editor at *Harvard Political Review.*

AS YOU READ, CONSIDER THE FOLLOWING QUESTIONS:
1. Which political party generally supports Trump's impeachment?
2. According to the author, are people making up their own minds about Trump's impeachment?
3. What do Democrats insist about this impeachment?

"The Politics of Impeachment: A Question of Legitimacy," by Kate Gundersen, *Harvard Political Review*, January 15, 2020. © 2020 The Harvard Political Review. All rights reserved. Reprinted with permission.

On December 18, 2019, the House of Representatives, under the direction of Speaker Nancy Pelosi (D-Calif.), voted to impeach President Donald Trump for abuse of power and obstruction of Congress. The move came after months of inquiry into Trump's dealings with Ukrainian President Volodymyr Zelensky, stemming from the press leak that a credible whistleblower had filed a complaint over the said dealings. With this inquiry has come a cascade of new information, yet public opinion about whether Trump should be impeached and/or removed from office has remained largely unchanged. Rather than independently making up their minds or changing them as the impeachment process evolves, many voters seem to view impeachment only through the stances taken by their preferred parties, leading them to focus not on the question of Trump's culpability but on the legitimacy of the impeachment process itself.

When it comes to Trump's impeachment, there is a strong and consistent partisan divide in public opinion. Since last October, 80 to 85 percent of Democrats have supported removing Trump from office, as compared to about 10 percent of Republicans. This gap correlates with how Democrats and Republicans feel about Trump: as of early December 2019, Trump only had a three percent approval rating among Democrats, while he had an 89 percent approval rating among Republicans. This correlation suggests that party views about Trump are playing a critical role in how people view the impeachment proceedings and the president's potential removal from office.

Furthermore, the consistency of this partisan divide in public opinion over impeachment indicates that the proceedings themselves have not changed partisans' minds. A November 19 NPR poll found that "65 [percent] of Americans say they can't imagine any information or circumstances during the impeachment inquiry where they might change their minds about their position on impeachment." As partisan viewpoints about impeachment were formed before the public hearings began, it seems that Americans are now relying heavily on their political predispositions and preferred party leaders' stances to shape their perspectives.

This consistent partisan divide reflects how the impeachment inquiry represents far more than a mere investigation; rather, it

Even as far back as the First Continental Congress, state delegates were given the rights to debate and equal representation.

represents a political spectacle, fueled largely by President Trump's efforts to discredit accusations about his potentially illegal conduct. Last November, he tweeted that the investigation was just "another Democrat Hoax"—representing one tweet of many that has shaped the public debate about impeachment. Calling the investigation a partisan-driven hoax calls into question its legitimacy. The legitimacy of the impeachment inquiry has become the main focus, distracting people from making an informed decision on the legality of the president's conduct.

House and Senate Republicans feed into Trump's claims that the impeachment process is illegitimate through their own partisan rhetoric. During the impeachment debate, Rep. Mike Kelly (R-Pa.) argued that Democrats "decided that the only way… [the] President doesn't get elected again is to impeach him." In the wake of House Democrats impeaching Trump, Senate Majority Leader Mitch McConnell (R-Ky.) deemed the decision reflected no more than "partisan passions." Both sentiments demonstrate that Republicans are pushing the narrative that the impeachment is a political attack by the Democrats, augmenting and seemingly legitimizing Trump's largely unsubstantiated and hotly contested claims. By putting up a united front behind Trump, Republicans are better able to defend him.

Across the aisle, Democrats are pushing back against the Republican narrative, claiming that the impeachment trial is legitimate and necessary. Speaker Pelosi summed up House Democrats' position when she opened the debate on impeachment, remarking that as members of Congress, all Representatives were "custodians of the Constitution" and that it was "tragic that the president's reckless actions make impeachment necessary." She concluded her address by telling her fellow Representatives that they were there "to defend democracy for the people." As Democrats feel that Trump's actions violated the Constitution, not impeaching him would represent a blow to the democratic process itself in their eyes. By emphasizing that impeachment is a necessary evil, stressing their impartiality, and upholding the legitimacy of the investigation, Democrats promote the idea that they are not impeaching Trump because they do not like him, but rather because he violated the law.

These different stances of the two parties on the nature of the impeachment proceedings have fueled divisions in public opinion: when the trial is legitimate for one party and illegitimate for the other, it is difficult for Democrats and Republicans to convince members of the opposite party that their side is correct. Furthermore, as Trump's approval rating among voters is deeply divided along party lines, it is easier for partisans to let their feelings about Trump as a president and person influence their feelings about the trial. If Republicans follow the views of their representatives, they are unlikely to support removing Trump—the trial itself seems to them like a partisan attack on a well-liked president. If Democrats follow the views of their representatives, they are likely to support removing Trump—the trial

FAST FACT

According to a Pew Research survey, around four in ten Republicans say that President Trump did something wrong but that it was not severe enough for impeachment and removal from office.

seems to them like a necessary check on an unpopular president. As a result, analyzing Trump's conduct takes a back seat to the question of whether or not he should be on trial at all.

As attention shifts to Trump's trial in January, the Republican-majority Senate is likely to vote to keep Trump in office. McConnell has gone so far as to say that he will work "in total coordination with the White House counsel" around organizing the trial, raising public concerns around the impartiality of the process. Sen. Lisa Murkowski (R-Ala.) has notably come out and said that she was "disturbed" by such an admission, but her Republican colleagues have stood by McConnell, suggesting that the current Republican narrative of Trump's victimization by the Democrats will remain salient until the trial's end. With the nation's leaders unable to find common ground, moreover, the trial will likely end without resolving the greater partisan divide it represents, potentially shaping voters' minds as they cast their ballots for the presidency and Congress in 2020.

EVALUATING THE AUTHOR'S ARGUMENTS:

In this viewpoint, author Kate Gundersen maps out a Democrat vs. Republican response to the first impeachment proceedings of Donald Trump. Choose a side and defend that side's response to the impeachment using details from this and other viewpoints.

The Constitution Does Not Detail the Impeachment Process

Jeannie Suk Gersen

"For most of us, judicial trials are the primary template for addressing wrongs against society, but what a fair impeachment trial looks like remains uncertain."

In the following viewpoint, Jeannie Suk Gersen analyzes the impeachment process used in the United States and details specifics of the process as it applied to US president Donald Trump's first impeachment. Gersen dives into the area of comparing this impeachment to court trials, the kind that most people are familiar with. Gersen details the public acknowledgements of senators that appear to be working outside of the traditionally defined oath to vote for Trump's acquittal. Jeannie Suk Gersen is a professor of law at Harvard Law School.

AS YOU READ, CONSIDER THE FOLLOWING QUESTIONS:
1. What do US senators do in a fair impeachment, according to the author?
2. What were the two articles of impeachment against President Trump in his first impeachment?
3. What is the voir dire process?

P rosecuting a case in front of a trial jury comes naturally to Representative Adam Schiff, a former federal prosecutor and the lead House manager in the impeachment trial of Donald Trump. Schiff has urged senators to think of themselves as "impartial jurors" with a constitutional responsibility "to hold a fair and thorough trial." But, more than a week into the trial, the question of the President's guilt of the charges of abuse of power and obstruction of Congress has been upstaged by suspense over whether the Senate will vote to allow the process for examining evidence that we ordinarily associate with a "trial"—particularly, hearing witness testimony. Once the allotted time for speeches by both sides has run, and after senators have a chance to put questions to each side, Democrats want the Senate to issue subpoenas for evidence, while Republicans aim to move immediately to a vote to acquit.

For most of us, judicial trials are the primary template for addressing wrongs against society, but what a fair impeachment trial looks like remains uncertain. The Constitution gives the Senate "the sole power to try all Impeachments" but doesn't specify what such a process consists of, other than that the senators "shall be on Oath or Affirmation," that conviction requires the votes of two-thirds of the members present, and that the Chief Justice must preside when the President is tried. As long as those rules are followed, it is unlikely that any Senate impeachment trial will ever be declared unconstitutional, regardless of how unfair it may seem. The key precedent is *Nixon v. United States*, a Supreme Court case on impeachment that, confusingly, didn't involve President Richard Nixon but, rather, a federal judge named Walter Nixon, whom the Senate convicted and removed in 1989, for giving false grand-jury testimony. In that case, the Court rejected the claim that the use of the term "try" in the phrase "try all Impeachments" means that a Senate impeachment trial must have some semblance of a judicial trial, including the hearing of evidence. (Kenneth Starr, then the Solicitor General, later the independent counsel in the investigation of Bill Clinton, and now a member or Trump's impeachment-trial defense team, won the case for the government.)

"Trial" for impeachment and "trial" elsewhere in the legal system are effectively homonyms, whose meanings may diverge as the Senate majority wishes. But the public's basic notions of procedural fairness, truth-seeking, and legitimacy are still stickily based on our expectations of trials in court—such as that witnesses will testify about the facts. So both parties have drawn on common ideas of what counts as a trial in order to support their arguments.

Trump's defense team is hammering on a lack of "due process" in the House proceedings that led to impeachment, likening them to the railroading of an innocent without a chance to be heard. The criminal-justice template exerts a powerful pull on the popular imagination, and the defense has argued, too, that, because the articles of impeachment against Trump, "abuse of power" and "obstruction of Congress," do not allege crimes—or, as the defense lawyer Alan Dershowitz has put it, "criminal-like conduct akin to treason and bribery"—they are illegitimate. (The articles of impeachment against Andrew Johnson, Nixon, and Clinton involved criminal wrongdoing.) This proffers a fig leaf for those senators who may believe that Trump did everything that is alleged but who still want to support acquittal. The solid weight of constitutional scholarship, however, has found that the Constitution's impeachment standard, "Treason, Bribery, or other high Crimes and Misdemeanors," clearly contemplates removal of a President who abuses the power of office for political gain, even if no crime was committed.

For Democrats, the news that John Bolton, Trump's former national-security adviser, has written in a book manuscript that the President told him that he wanted to withhold aid to Ukraine until it agreed to investigate Joe and Hunter Biden, has bolstered the case that witness testimony should be part of any "fair and thorough trial." Liberals also have complained about Senate Majority Leader Mitch McConnell's commitment to conduct the Senate trial in "total coördination" with the White House. Early this month, Public Citizen, a consumer-rights advocacy group, filed an ethics complaint against McConnell, focussing on his December, 2019, statement, "I am not an impartial juror. This is a political process." (Senator Lindsey Graham similarly stated, "I'm not trying to pretend to be a fair juror here.") The nub of the complaint is that McConnell confessed intent to violate the oath that has been required of senators in impeachment trials since that of Andrew Johnson, in 1868: that they "will do impartial justice according to the Constitution and laws."

Decision-makers' attempt to be impartial is crucial to the legitimacy of the legal system. A jury trial, for example, is preceded by a voir-dire process, in which potential jurors are questioned on their ability to be impartial, so that those seemingly unable can be weeded out. But if a similar voir-dire process had preceded Trump's impeachment trial, few members would have remained. The meaning of "impartial justice" in this context is different from whatever impartiality we purport to expect from jurors. But, as Public Citizen's complaint explains, while we don't expect senators to "pretend to be a blank slate evaluating impeachment evidence for the first time," the oath still obligates them not to enter with "a locked-in conclusion based on partisanship, personal allegiance or political calculations." Presumably, that's what Schiff meant in reminding senators of their duty to "to hold a fair and thorough trial."

It's useful to recall that Senate Democrats once were reluctant to adopt the "juror" mind-set. During the impeachment trial of President Bill Clinton, Republicans pushing for conviction characterized senators as "jurors." Democrats vigorously objected, even asking Chief Justice William Rehnquist to weigh in. As Senator

Special Counsel Robert Mueller is sworn in before testifying to the House Judiciary Committee in 2019. Mueller led the investigation into possible Russian interference in the 2016 election.

Tom Harkin, Democrat of Iowa, who supported Clinton's acquittal, argued, "Regular jurors cannot overrule the judge. Not so here. Regular jurors do not decide what evidence should be heard or the standards of evidence, nor do they decide on witnesses or what witnesses shall be called. Not so here. Regular jurors do not decide when a trial is to be ended. Not so here." The Chief Justice ruled that counsel should "refrain from referring to the senators as jurors." He explained, "The Senate is not simply a jury—it is a court in this case."

Because a trial jury's limited role is to find the facts—and the Democrats' case is rather damning on the facts—it also serves Trump's lawyers to liken the Senate's impartiality obligation not to that of a trial jury but to that of a "high court," which reviews legal mistakes in the proceedings of lower courts and invalidates decisions resulting from those errors. On Monday, Starr urged the Senate to do just that with the articles of impeachment, saying that the House had conducted an impeachment process riddled with procedural mistakes—namely, by failing to provide "due process for the accused"—and had thereby "inadvertently pointed this court to an exit ramp," through acquittal.

At the heart of it, whether a President will be removed turns "primarily on whether Congress thinks it is good or bad for the country that he or she should be permitted to remain as chief executive," as Frank O. Bowman III puts it in his book, "High Crimes and Misdemeanors: A History of Impeachment for the Age of Trump." By constitutional design, the decision lies with a political body that is not as insulated from public opinion as the judiciary is expected to be, but that is supposed to be less immediately responsive to constituents' demands than the House. Both sides in Trump's impeachment trial are banking on the idea that challenging the process will help their side. Despite the utter lack of suspense as to acquittal along party lines, Democrats can benefit by attributing that eventuality to the Senate's refusal of fair process. And because Republicans also know acquittal is assured, notwithstanding the President's perfidious conduct, they save face by casting acquittal as the response to the House's denial of fair process. Perhaps what that confirms is that the underlying facts of Trump's wrongdoing and his denial of them are less compelling fodder in the impeachment court of public opinion than the conduct of Congress itself.

EVALUATING THE AUTHOR'S ARGUMENTS:

In this viewpoint, author Jeannie Suk Gersen reports that Senator Mitch McConnell and Senator Lindsey Graham freely admit that they will not be impartial or free jurors in the impeachment trial of President Donald Trump. How can they publicly admit to not following the oath that senators are required to abide by during impeachment proceedings?

The Impeachment Process Is Unfair

"Election Day is now less than one year away. Let [voters] judge if President Donald Trump should be removed from office."

Rachel Alexander

In the following viewpoint, Rachel Alexander presents the conditions of President Donald Trump's impeachment. Alexander clearly argues from a conservative viewpoint, contending that Trump did not commit offenses worthy of impeachment. The author insists that the left went after conservatives for no impeachable reason. Rachel Alexander is a conservative political columnist, and a senior editor at the *Stream*.

AS YOU READ, CONSIDER THE FOLLOWING QUESTIONS:

1. According to the author, why did Donald Trump's impeachment take place?
2. Why doesn't the author think that "quid pro quo" is not impeachable?
3. As explained in the viewpoint, who will stop Donald Trump from being removed from office?

"The Unfair Impeachment Process," by Rachel Alexander, *The Stream*, November 4, 2019. Reprinted by permission.

Is going to the polls and voting a more effective and fair way to remove a president from the White House than the current impeachment process?

I've been a prosecutor. I know what prosecutable crimes look like. And I can tell you Donald Trump didn't commit one. There are no grounds for impeaching the president. What's the point of the elaborate process now going in Congress? To get anything the Democrats can get. They want to defeat the man they couldn't defeat in a fair election.

As Representative Tom Cole of Oklahoma, the top Republican on the Rules Committee, said, the process is geared to "a preordained result." It's not about the law. It's about using the law to get a political enemy.

Behind Closed Doors

House Democrats are conducting the impeachment proceedings behind closed doors, only allowing members of the three committees involved to attend. Why would they do that? Are they discussing national secrets? No. They're doing it to avoid public scrutiny.

Closed doors decrease the chance the public will call out their unfair tactics.

Democrats are refusing to let witnesses favorable to Trump testify in the closed door hearings. Nor are they letting Trump's legal team cross-examine witnesses. House Intelligence Committee Chairman Adam Schiff (D-Calif.), who leads the impeachment inquiry, is halting lines of questioning he doesn't like from GOP representatives who are part of the hearing. This is unfair because the whole picture isn't being portrayed. Trump deserves due process and a fair, impartial proceeding. At the very least, he is due the same somber, bipartisan treatment and procedures afforded Richard Nixon and Bill Clinton.

The Democrats in the House will eventually start public hearings. They passed an impeachment inquiry resolution on Thursday to authorize them. But it doesn't ensure minority subpoena power or the release of transcripts. It doesn't equally allocate staffing between parties. It doesn't allow Trump's lawyers to be present to question witnesses and present evidence. Again, due process isn't part of this process.

Quid Pro Quo Isn't a Crime

The impeachment effort was hurriedly launched because someone claimed that Trump had engaged in a quid pro quo with Ukrainian president Volodymyr Zelenskyy. The anonymous "whistleblower" made his charges to Schiff.

The informant claimed that Trump threatened in a phone call to withhold aid from Ukraine in exchange for a political favor. Trump allegedly wanted Zelenskyy to find out why the prosecution was dropped against Joe Biden's son's business dealings.

Then Trump unexpectedly released the transcript of the call. Everyone could see what he actually said, and it's clear he did not ask for a quid pro quo. Trump mentioned at the beginning that the US had been very good to Ukraine. Later he asks Zelenskyy to look into the dropped

FAST FACT

Quid pro quo is a Latin phrase that means "something for something" or "this for that."

prosecution. There is clearly no correlation between the two. The whistleblower's depiction was fiction.

Troubling Inquiry

It is troubling that an impeachment inquiry would be opened when it's not clear what crime has allegedly been committed. Consider the Clinton impeachment, where Whitewater prosecutor Ken Starr presented Congress with 11 clear possible grounds for impeachment. Here, the whistleblower fretted about possible campaign finance violations, which the DOJ quickly knocked down.

Whatever the vague phrase "quid pro quo" means, it is not a crime. Presidents have always asked governments we aid to do something in exchange for that aid. That can include investigating Americans possibly committing crimes abroad. Here, President Trump was looking for assistance in investigating the extent of Ukraine's admitted role in interfering in the 2016 election. He was also curious about Biden in the wake of Biden publicly boasting about withholding $1.5 billion in aid to Ukraine if they didn't fire the prosecutor investigating a corrupt company called Burisma. Burisma happened to be putting millions into the pockets of Biden's son.

So what do the Democrats do? They expand the definition of the offenses for which Trump can be tried. Ezra Klein, arguing at Vox, asserts that the definition of "high crimes and misdemeanors" does not necessarily mean a crime. The article's subtitle claims: "Abuse of power may not be a crime. But it is absolutely a high crime and misdemeanor."

In 1828, Webster's Dictionary defined it in 1828 as "ill behavior; evil conduct; fault; mismanagement." Klein claims that it "wasn't a light crime, but an abusive act." Furthermore, a 2015 Congressional Research Service report surveyed every House impeachment in American history. It concluded that "less than a third have specifically invoked a criminal statute or used the term 'crime.'"

Definition of High Crimes and Misdemeanors

Klein analyzes the definition provided by various legal scholars. But they undermine his claim. The scholars address more serious actions than Trump's phone call — even if Trump had done something wrong.

One describes it as offenses that "so seriously threaten the order of political society as to make pestilent and dangerous the continuance in power of their perpetrator." Another pair of legal scholars said that "impeachable offenses involve corruption, betrayal or an abuse of power that … risk grave injury to the nation."

Another aspect of political targeting is to go after the people beneath the target. It makes the target look bad. Even better from the prosecutor's point, sometimes the underlings will turn on the target. They're usually not powerful, wealthy and connected unlike the target so it's easier to take them down. The bar came after me because I was an underling. Their real target was my former boss.

Similarly, the left is going after Trump's private attorney Rudy Giuliani. New York prosecutors are looking into his dealings with Ukraine. This could lead to his disbarment. Going after people in politics who are lawyers is one way the left targets conservatives. State bars are generally controlled by people on the left, so it is easy to get them to go after conservatives. It's no coincidence the left chose him to investigate. His law license makes him a ripe target.

The Outcome Is Obvious

House Democrats will impeach Trump. They control the House. They have the votes. We've seen this type of witch hunt play out all too often. It's all about insinuation. They don't have a real crime to pin on Trump. Do they give up? No. They just act like he did something awful.

Fortunately, wiser heads in the Republican-controlled Senate should stop the process from removing Trump. The Democrats will never get enough votes to convict. They need 67. That means getting at least 16 Republicans to vote with them. That's almost impossible.

Here's a better idea. In fact, it's such a good idea the Framers put it into the Constitution. Election Day is now less than one year away. We, the People will again go to the polls. Let them judge if President Donald Trump should be removed from office. And in the meantime, the House can finally get to the business of the people rather than the business of overthrowing the 2016 election.

EVALUATING THE AUTHOR'S ARGUMENTS:

Viewpoint author Rachel Alexander argues that voters should determine the president's fate. What do you think she will write about Donald Trump being voted out of office in the 2020 election? What do you think she will write about Trump's attempts to disallow votes in the states that put Biden over the top to win the presidential election?

Viewpoint
5

Public Opinion Impacts Impeachment

William A. Galston

> *"A president's standing with the American people as the impeachment inquiry proceeds makes a big difference."*

In the following viewpoint, William A. Galston analyzes the part that public opinion plays in the impeachment of a US president. Galston details how public opinion affected the impeachment processes of Richard Nixon and Bill Clinton. He then uses the same reasoning to highlight issues of public opinion in the impeachment of Donald Trump. William A. Galston is a senior fellow at the Brookings Institution. He writes a weekly column for the *Wall Street Journal*.

AS YOU READ, CONSIDER THE FOLLOWING QUESTIONS:
1. How did public opinion affect Richard Nixon?
2. How was public opinion different when Bill Clinton was facing impeachment, according to the author?
3. According to Galston, which four Senate Republicans may not stick up for Trump?

"Impeachment and Public Opinion: Three Key Indicators to Watch," by William A. Galston, The Brookings Institution, September 27, 2019. Reprinted by permission.

T here have been two serious efforts in the past half-century to impeach and remove a US president from office. The first, which ended in 1974, led to the resignation of its target—President Richard Nixon. The second, which began in 1998 against President Bill Clinton, led to the resignation of the man who had orchestrated the effort—House Speaker Newt Gingrich.

In the former case, opinion shifted steadily against President Nixon and in favor of removing him from office as the public reacted to swirling events at both ends of Pennsylvania Avenue and learned more about the details of the Watergate affair. In the latter, new information had almost no impact on the views of the people about removing President Clinton, which they opposed from the beginning of this episode to the very end.

Now we have entered the early phase of a third impeachment and removal effort, this time directed against President Donald Trump. Will it lead to triumph or disaster for Democrats? Will it lead to the end of Mr. Trump's presidency or pave the way for his reelection? We do not know. But history gives us clues about what to watch for along the way.

First, a president's standing with the American people as the impeachment inquiry proceeds makes a big difference. As the Watergate hearings unfolded in the summer of 1973, soon followed by the infamous Saturday night massacre in the fall, President Nixon's job approval fell steadily from 50% in the late spring of 1973 to just 24% at the beginning of 1974. During the next eight months, culminating in Mr. Nixon's resignation, it barely budged. In short, Nixon was gravely damaged politically long before the House of Representatives voted to impeach him on three counts in July.

By contrast, President Clinton's job approval, which stood above 60% at the beginning of 1998, never fell below 60% during that year, spiked upward to 73% at the end of the year, and stood in the high-60s as the Senate failed to approve either of the articles of impeachment in January of 1999.

A second key indicator is public support for the impeachment effort itself. Public support for impeaching and removing President Nixon rose steadily through 1973, roughly doubling by the end of the year, and rose another 20 points from January to August of 1974.

IMPEACHMENT PROCEDURE

PRESIDENT COMMITS IMPEACHABLE ACT

MEMBER OF HOUSE OF REPRESENTATIVES INTRODUCES A RESOLUTION OF IMPEACHMENT

THE HOUSE INVESTIGATES CLAIMS OF WRONGDOING

THE HOUSE VOTES IN FAVOR OF IMPEACHMENT

THE SENATE HOLDS A TRIAL

SENATE HOLDS A VOTE TO CONVICT THE PRESIDENT

IF GUILTY - PRESIDENT IS REMOVED FROM OFFICE

IF NOT GUILTY - PRESIDENT REMAINS IN OFFICE

The impeachment process includes standard steps, but it does not account for the impact of public opinion.

In contrast, again, public support for impeaching and removing Bill Clinton did not budge through the summer and fall of 1998, despite congressional hearings, the explosive special prosecutor's report, and approval of impeachment articles. On August 8, according to Gallup, 34% of Americans supported impeachment and 63% opposed it. The December 12 survey, which asked the same question word for word, found the identical result—34% in favor, 63% opposed. In the eyes of the American people, Clinton's accusers had failed to make their case against him.

A New York Times/CBS News poll conducted after the House impeachment hearings and votes also found that these events had "no effect" on the public's view of the proceedings against Mr. Clinton. Even after approval of articles of impeachment, nearly two-thirds said that the Senate should not put the president on trial but should instead work out a compromise, such as a formal censure. If a trial occurred, 68% said that the Senate should not remove him from office.

This is not to say that the public doubted the truth of the accusations against President Clinton. By the end of 1998, a majority of the American people had decided that Mr. Clinton had lied under oath, engaged in illegal acts, and abused the powers of his office. But as a December 1998 Gallup report concluded, the majority did not believe that these offenses "[rose] to the level of being impeachable."

A third key indicator is the extent of bipartisan support for impeachment in the House of Representatives. When the House Judiciary Committee voted on impeaching President Nixon, 6 out of 17 Republicans supported the charge that he had obstructed justice, and 7 agreed with the charge that he had abused the powers of his office. This presaged the dramatic trip of a Republican senatorial delegation headed by Barry Goldwater to the Oval Office to inform President Nixon that support for him had collapsed, even among members of his own party. Informed that he would lose an impeachment vote and that the Senate would vote to convict him, Nixon resigned before either vote happened.

Events played out very differently in 1998. When the full House voted on articles of impeachment, only 5 Democrats out of 205 voted to support any of these articles. When the Senate voted on the two articles that had received a majority in the House, no Democrat supported either one, a result foreshadowed by the sharp partisan divisions in the House.

Measured against these three key indicators—presidential job approval, public support for impeaching and removing the president, and bipartisan support in Congress, where do matters stand as efforts to impeach President Trump begin in earnest?

Presidential Job Approval

An NPR/PBS/Marist poll conducted after Tuesday's revelations but before the release of the whistleblower's complaint puts approval of President Trump among registered voters at 45%, within the narrow band it has occupied for most of his presidency. Republican support for the president still stands at 90%. Two other polls, HuffPost/YouGov and Politico/Morning Consult, also found presidential approval remaining largely unchanged, with Republicans standing staunchly behind the president. If neither of these numbers changes as this saga unfolds, the Democrats will likely suffer the same fate as did the Republicans two decades ago.

Support for Impeachment

The NPR/PBS/Marist survey shows a country sharply divided—along partisan lines—on the merits of proceeding. Overall, 49% support impeachment while 46% oppose it, figures that include 88% Democratic support and 93% Republican opposition. (In evidence of partisan intensity, 61% of Democrats "strongly" approve, while 80% of Republicans strongly disapprove.) 82% of Democrats regard this as a very serious matter; 85% of Republicans dismiss it as pure politics. Still, there are signs that the Republican wall of opposition may not be completely impregnable: 52% of Republicans think that the whistleblower should testify before Congress, and 27% regard the president's telephone call requesting Ukrainian cooperation with an inquiry into Joe Biden's conduct as a serious matter warranting further investigation.

A HuffPost/YouGov poll taken between Tuesday night and Thursday morning sheds some early light on the dynamics of a rapidly changing situation. There has been a modest uptick in public support for impeachment, from 42% to 47%. This gain is almost entirely attributable to increased support among Democrats, which has risen from 74% to 81% during the past two weeks. Support among Independents has remained stable in the mid-30s while declining among Republicans from 16% to 11%.

A Politico/Morning Consult poll, also taken between Tuesday and Thursday, found similar results. Although support for impeachment rose by 7 points, most of the increase is attributable to a 13-point jump among Democrats, and the country remains divided on the matter, 43 to 43, with 13% unsure.

Support for Impeachment in the House

At this point, sentiment among House members divides starkly along party lines. More than 90% of House Democrats have indicated their support for an inquiry that almost certainly will culminate in articles of impeachment, while as of now, not a single House Republicans has come close to voicing support.

As many commentators have noted, a public statement by newly-elected moderate Democrats from swing districts helped crystallize pro-impeachment sentiment within the party. Based on a close analysis of the 1998 and 2000 election results, veteran analyst Ron Brownstein concludes that House Republicans who defied sentiments in their districts by voting to impeach President Clinton paid at most a modest price, suggesting that moderate Democrats may not suffer much either in 2020. On the other hand, the Monmouth survey looked at swing counties, decided by less than 10 points in 2016, and found that only 32% of voters in these contested areas supported the impeachment and removal of President Trump, with 60% opposed, while just 22% thought that the Senate was likely to remove the president after the House voted to impeach him.

The evidence suggests that these voters are right about the Senate's likely response to articles of impeachment. Senate Republicans have remained mostly in lockstep behind Mr. Trump since he assumed office. Of the 53 Senate Republicans, 45 hail from solidly red states. Of the remaining 8, just 4—Susan Collins of Maine, Cory Gardner of Colorado, Martha McSally of Arizona, and Tom Tillis of North Carolina—will face the voters in 2020. Most Senate Republicans need fear primary challenges but not serious general election contests. Unless sentiment about President Trump shifts sharply among Republicans in their states in the coming months, their political calculus points toward sticking with him. The imponderable factor in this equation is the number of Republican senators who will decide to buck the preferences of their supporters in favor of what they have decided is the constitutionally required course of action.

Persuading the public to support impeaching and removing a president is a two-step process. The public must be convinced that the charges are true—and that they are weighty enough to justify overturning the results of a presidential election. Mr. Nixon's accusers met both these tests, and he was forced to resign. By contrast, Mr. Clinton's accusers met the first test but not the second. As the Senate trial began, 79% of Americans thought the president had committed perjury and 53% that he had obstructed justice, but only 4 in 10 believed that either charge warranted Clinton's removal from office. The Senate vote fell far short on both counts of the indictment, and their target served out the rest of his term as a popular chief executive.

As the impeachment effort against President Trump gets underway, the American people are divided on both these tests, and his accusers must meet a weighty burden of proof. It remains to be seen whether the Democrats' announced determination to proceed swiftly to impeachment will give the people enough time to assimilate new information and perhaps change their minds.

EVALUATING THE AUTHOR'S ARGUMENTS:

Viewpoint author William A. Galston examines an important idea about presidential impeachment involving public opinion. Using details from any viewpoint in chapter 3, compare the ideas of fairness in impeachment to public opinion about impeachment.

Facts About Impeachment

Editor's note: These facts can be used in reports to add credibility when making important points or claims.

Actors in the United States Government During Impeachment

Members of the Senate: Individual members vote whether to convict and remove a sitting president from office at the end of the impeachment trial.

Members of the House of Representatives: Individual members vote for or against articles of impeachment, which leads to a Senate trial.

Constitutional Indications for Impeachment

September 17, 1787: The members of the Constitutional Convention finally approved a draft of the US Constitution, which included the articles pertaining to impeachment.

Article I, Section 2: Gives the power of impeachment to the US House of Representatives.

Article I, Section 3: Gives the Senate the power to try all impeachments.

Article II, Section 4: Defines who can be impeached.

Article II, Section 4: Impeachable crimes include treason, bribery, and other high crimes and misdemeanors.

Intention of America's Founding Fathers

To remind both the country and the president that he is not above the law.

To deter abuses of power.

To provide a fair and reliable method to resolve suspicions about misconduct.

Key US Impeachments

July 7, 1797: First impeachment in the United States. William Blount was impeached on charges of conspiring to assist Great Britain's attempt to seize territories in Florida and Louisiana. Charges were dismissed, but Blount was expelled from the US Senate.

February 24, 1868: First US president to be impeached. Andrew Johnson was impeached on charges of violating the Tenure of Office Act. Johnson removed Secretary of War Edwin Stanton (served as President Abraham Lincoln's secretary of war) from office. Johnson was ultimately acquitted.

July 1974: The House of Representatives' Judiciary Committee approved three articles of impeachment against Richard M. Nixon. Before being charged by members of the House, Nixon resigned from office, so he was never actually impeached.

December 19, 1998: President William J. Clinton was impeached on charges of lying under oath and obstruction of justice. He was acquitted.

December 18, 2019: President Donald J. Trump was impeached on charges of abuse of power and obstruction of Congress. He was acquitted.

January 13, 2021: President Donald J. Trump was impeached for a second time, just one week before leaving office. The president was acquitted for the second time.

Impeachments Outside the United States

In general, other world countries have their own methods for impeachment of a leader.

2015: Impeachment of Otto Perez Molina in Guatemala, convicted and removed from office.

2016: Impeachment of Dilma Rousseff in Brazil, convicted and removed from office.

2017: Impeachment of Park Geun-hye in South Korea, convicted and removed from office.

Organizations to Contact

The editors have compiled the following list of organizations concerned with the issues debated in this book. The descriptions are derived from materials provided by the organizations. All have publications or information available for interested readers. The list was compiled on the date of publication of the present volume; the information provided here may change. Be aware that many organizations take several weeks or longer to respond to inquiries, so allow as much time as possible for the receipt of requested materials.

The Brookings Institution

1775 Massachusetts Avenue NW
Washington, DC 20036
(202) 797-6000
email: use links on contact page
website: www.brookings.edu/
The Brookings Institution is a nonprofit organization dedicated to research that leads to new ideas to benefit society. Read articles and listen to podcasts for information all about impeachment.

Citizens for Responsibility and Ethics in Washington (CREW)

1101 K Street NW
Suite 201
Washington, DC 20005
(202) 408-5565
email: info@citizensforethics.org
website: www.citizensforethics.org
Founded in 2003, CREW acts in a nonpartisan way with in-depth investigations and bold actions and targets government officials who put personal gain and special interest above the common good. Read articles, sign up for a newsletter, and follow the organization on Twitter to be informed about corruption and misdeeds of public people.

Congressional Research Service (CRS)

101 Independence Avenue SE
Washington, DC 20540
(202) 707-5000
email: www.loc.gov/crsinfo/contact/
website: www.loc.gov/crsinfo/about/
This US governmental service within the Library of Congress provides reliable and accurate legislative research that is timely. A search provides information across federal agencies.

Independence Hall Association (IHA)

Carpenters' Hall
320 Chestnut Street
Philadelphia, PA 19106
(800) 732-0999
email: www.ushistory.org/contact.htm
website: //store.ushistory.org/
The IHA is an organization dedicated to US history. Trust this website as an online source for reliable information on all topics of United States history. Watch full videos of history centered around Philadelphia, PA. Access primary documents such as Abraham Lincoln's Emancipation Proclamation, the US Constitution, George Washington's farewell speech, and much more. This is an all-around great historical resource.

National Conference of State Legislatures (NCSL)

444 North Capitol Street NW
Suite 515
Washington, DC 20001
(202) 624-5400
email: use contact page of website
website: www.ncsl.org/
The NCSL represents the legislatures of the states, territories, and commonwealths of the United States. This organization helps states deal with the federal government and provides information in the form of articles, blogs, podcasts, and more. Find information about impeachment on its site.

Pew Research Center
1615 L Street NW
Suite 800
Washington, DC 20036
(202) 419-4300
email: info@pewresearch.org
www.pewresearch.org/
Pew Research Center is a nonpartisan agency intent on providing facts and information on a wide range of topics important for the public. It conducts polling, informational surveys, social science research, and more to inform interested parties through reports, surveys, and data-driven analysis. Obtain information through reading articles, studying charts and graphs, following its blog and other social media, and signing up for a weekly newsletter.

Project on Government Oversight (POGO)
1100 G Street NW
Suite 500
Washington, DC 20005-7433
(202) 347-1122
email: info@pogo.org
website: www.pogo.org
The POGO group is a watchdog agency intent on investigating and exposing corruption, abuse of power, and government wrongdoing. This site contains a wide range of searchable information, but more importantly, the organization has a collection and series section with one theme dedicated to impeachment.

For Further Reading

Books

Allen, John. *The Impeachment of President Donald Trump*. San Diego, CA: Reference Point Press, Inc., 2021. The election of the forty-fifth US president took many by surprise. But Donald J. Trump did take office and served for four years. This book details how he was impeached and subsequently acquitted.

Cohen, Daniel. *The Impeachment of William Jefferson Clinton*. Minneapolis, MN: Twenty-First Century Books, 2000. Learn all about the events leading up to the impeachment of William J. Clinton, forty-second president of the United States.

Cruden, Alex. *Watergate*. New York, NY: Greenhaven, 2012. Richard M. Nixon, the thirty-seventh president of the United States, resigned before he could be impeached. Read about Watergate, the affair that ended this presidency.

Edwards, Sue Bradford. *The Impeachment of Donald Trump*. Minneapolis, MN: Abdo Publishing, 2021. Including a brief overview of the process of impeachment, this book includes all the facts about the impeachment of President Donald J. Trump.

Jacobson, Bray. *The US Constitution*. New York, NY: Gareth Stevens Publishing, 2018. Delve into this book to understand all about the US Constitution, including the section pertaining to impeachment.

McPherson, Stephanie Sammartino. *Political Parties: From Nominations to Victory Celebrations*. Minneapolis, MN: Lerner Publications, 2016. Two major political parties operate in the US. Find out why, the key issues involved, how these parties influence candidates and elections, and more.

Osborne, Linda Barrett. *Guardians of Liberty: Freedom of the Press and the Nature of News*. New York, NY: Abrams Books for Young Readers, 2020. In a democracy, the press and media need to be able to freely report on issues. They must not be vilified and tagged as untrustworthy, which has been an important point during the 2020 impeachment proceedings.

Reston, Dominick. *Donald Trump: 45th US President.* San Diego, CA: Reference Point Press, Inc., 2017. This biography shines a spotlight on the life, career, and later political aspirations of Donald J. Trump, the forty-fifth president of the United States. Learn all about this unconventional president who was impeached and acquitted.

Periodicals and Internet Sources

Allen, Jonathan. "The Trump Chaos Theory for How to Beat Impeachment," NBC News Now, November 5, 2019. https://www.nbcnews.com/politics/trump-impeachment-inquiry/trump-chaos-theory-how-beat-impeachment-n1076796

Allyn, Bobby. "White House Says President Trump Won't Participate in Wednesday Impeachment Hearing," NPR, December 1, 2019. https://www.npr.org/2019/12/01/783989343/as-impeachment-inquiry-moves-to-judiciary-committee-republicans-attack-the-proce

Dershowitz, Alan. "A Partisan Impeachment Vote Is Exactly What the Framers Feared," The Hill, November 1, 2019. https://thehill.com/opinion/judiciary/468483-a-partisan-impeachment-vote-is-exactly-what-the-framers-feared

Eschner, Kat. "Presidents Can Be Impeached Because Benjamin Franklin Thought It Was Better Than Assassination," Smithsonian, December 19, 2016. https://www.smithsonianmag.com/smart-news/american-presidents-can-be-impeached-because-benjamin-franklin-thought-it-was-better-assassination-180961500/

Fandos, Nicholas. "Trump Impeached for Abuse of Power and Obstruction of Congress," *New York Times*, August 25, 2020. https://www.nytimes.com/2019/12/18/us/politics/trump-impeached.html

Herb, Jeremy. "How Each Senator Voted on Impeachment," CNN, February 5, 2020. https://www.cnn.com/interactive/2020/02/politics/senate-impeachment-vote/

Kelly, Jane. "Constitutional Scholar Explains How Impeachment Works in a Hyper-Partisan Era," *UVAToday*, September 26, 2019. https://news.virginia.edu/content/constitutional-scholar-explains-how-impeachment-works-hyper-partisan-era

Montanaro, Domenico. "Poll: Americans Overwhelmingly Say Impeachment Proceedings Won't Change Their Minds," NPR, November 19, 2019. https://www.npr.org/2019/11/19/780540637 /poll-americans-overwhelmingly-say-impeachment-hearings -wont-change-their-minds

Presser, Stephen B. "There Is No Good Case for Impeachment," American Greatness, November 26, 2019. https://amgreatness .com/2019/11/26/there-is-no-good-case-for-impeachment/

Rapoza, Kenneth. "Facts and Fictions Behind the Pending Impeachment of Brazil's President Dilma," *Forbes*, June 6, 2016. https:// www.forbes.com/sites/kenrapoza/2016/06/06/facts-and-fictions -behind-the-pending-impeachment-of-brazils-president -dilma/?sh=55d93e759220

Santucci, Jeanine. "It's Been One Year Since the Trump Impeachment Began. These Are the Major Moments of His Presidency Since," *USA Today*, September 24, 2020. https://www.usatoday.com/story /news/politics/2020/09/24/one-year-since-trump-impeachment -began-major-moments-presidency/5770781002/

Savage, David G. "Chief Justice Roberts Presided Impartially, Yet Left Questions Whether Trump's Trial Was a Fair One," *Los Angeles Times*, February 5, 2020. https://www.latimes.com/politics/story /2020-02-05/chief-justice-john-roberts-senate-impeachment -trial-impartiality

Savoy, Paul. "An Impeachment Trial Without Witnesses Would Be Unconstitutional," *Atlantic*, January 23, 2020. https://www.theatlantic .com/ideas/archive/2020/01/impeachment-trial-without-witness es-would-be-unconstitutional/605332/

Schaul, Kevin. "How the Senate Voted on the Trump Impeachment Charges," *Washington Post*, February 5, 2020. https://www .washingtonpost.com/graphics/2020/politics/senate -impeachment-votes-live-tracking/

Sherman, Mark. "AP Explains: What a Trump Impeachment Trial Might Look Like," AP, December 16, 2019. https://apnews.com /article/e10d1b2095952eae49cdaebbf9fb19a9

Togoh, Isabel. "Here's How the World Reacted to President Trump's Impeachment," *Forbes*, December 19, 2019. https://www.forbes

.com/sites/isabeltogoh/2019/12/19/heres-how-the-world
-reacted-to-president-trumps-impeachment/?sh=6ef625de1c03

Wolfe, Jan. "Explainer: How Trump's Impeachment Trial Would Differ
from a Criminal One," Reuters, December 31, 2019. https://www
.reuters.com/article/us-usa-trump-impeachment-trials-explaine
/explainer-how-trumps-impeachment-trial-would-differ-from-a
-criminal-one-idUSKBN1YZ0PT

Websites

History, Art & Archives: US House of Representatives (history.house
.gov/Institution/Impeachment/Impeachment-List/) This site provides a short article of interest about impeachment. It also includes
a graphic showing all the cases of impeachment in the US.

United States Senate (www.senate.gov/reference/Index/Impeachment
.htm) This site is a reference providing information about the US
Senate. This page is a direct link to information about the impeachment process.

US History.org (www.ushistory.org/) The Independence Hall Association (IHA) sponsors this website. The organization is dedicated
to bringing factual information about all aspects of United States
history to interested readers.

Index

Picture Credits

Cover bakdc/Shutterstock.com; p. 10 Jewel Samad/AFP via Getty Images; p. 14 JPLDesigns/iStock/Getty Images Plus; p. 21 Pgiam/E+/Getty Images; p. 26 Courtesy of the National Archives/Newsmakers/Hulton Archive/Getty Images; p. 32 George Bridges/AFP via Getty Images; p. 38 Owen Franken/Corbis via Getty Images; p. 44 Robert Alexander/Getty Images; p. 47 Mandel Ngan/AFP via Getty Images; p. 50 Joseph Prezioso/AFP via Getty Images; p. 57 Mark Wilson/Getty Images; p. 61 Drew Angerer/Getty Images; p. 66 Olivier Douliery–Pool/Getty Images; p. 72 Erin Kirkland/Bloomberg via Getty Images; p. 77 DNY59/E+/Getty Images; p. 80 Pict Rider/iStock/Getty Images Plus; p. 86 Keith Lance/DigitalVision Vectors/Getty Images; p. 93 Win McNamee/Getty Images; p. 96 Karen Bleier/AFP via Getty Images; p. 103 Inspiring/Shutterstock.com.